SIMPLE GOALKEEPING
MADE SPECTACULAR

Graham Joyce is the author of a collection of short stories and 16 novels, most recently *Memoirs of a Master Forger* (under the pen-name William Heaney). He was presented with the World Fantasy Award for his novel *The Facts of Life*, and he has won the British Fantasy Award for Best Novel an unprecedented four times. His work has been translated into more than 20 languages and has earned him several international awards. In 2009, he was awarded a prestigious O. Henry Prize for his short story 'The Ordinary Soldier of the Queen'.

SIMPLE GOALKEEPING MADE SPECTACULAR

A RIOTOUS FOOTBALLING MEMOIR ABOUT THE LONELIEST POSITION ON THE FIELD

GRAHAM JOYCE

MAINSTREAM
PUBLISHING

EDINBURGH AND LONDON

**TO MY DAD, BILL JOYCE,
AND TO MY BROTHERS, MARTIN AND DAVID**

First published in Great Britain in 2009 by
MAINSTREAM PUBLISHING COMPANY
(EDINBURGH) LTD
7 Albany Street
Edinburgh EH1 3UG

ISBN 9781845964474

A catalogue record for this book is available
from the British Library

Typeset in Minion and Trade Gothic

Printed in Great Britain by
CPI Mackays of Chatham Ltd, Chatham, ME5 8TD

I t's mid-January. The sky is a mucky grey and it's hammering it down outside, though there are irritating patches of eggshell blue towards the south. I don't want a break in the clouds, I want it to lash down because we've got a game tomorrow and I want it to be called off. We're awaiting a groundsman's decision, apparently.

I don't even remember who we're playing and I can't be arsed to check back through my emails to find out, but the opposition will be just like us: a bunch of chronically unskilled middle-aged no-hopers who should know better, who should have hung up their boots; a bunch of silly old farts with grey hair and outrageous fantasies about their own playing abilities.

The reason I don't want to be involved is that I've got a touch of the flu. There will be mud. There will be more rain. It's as cold as a well-digger's arse out there and if there's no action in my goalmouth I'll be freezing and miserable. On the other goalkeeper's glove, if there *is* plenty of action, I'll be muddy and freezing and miserable. And probably depressed.

I play for England, by the way. Oh, all right, England Writers, if you must split hairs. I'm goalkeeper. Mudlark. Sandboy.

Who is this groundsman we're waiting on? Well, you can depend on his name being Maurice. All groundsmen are cloth-capped pensioners called Maurice. They are all self-important retired engineers, or superannuated shopkeepers and being a groundsman is a part-time job they imagine keeps them fit and involved in the game. Just to enrage you further, they wear those Wellington boots with the rubber turned over halfway up the calf, so you can see a sweat-stained little band of dirty canvas.

Why this vitriol against groundsmen? I'll tell you. And, as my uncle Harold used to say, I'll tell you *for nothing*.

I've hated groundsmen since I was 16 years old and I played for my school, Nicholas Chamberlaine, a giant factory-fodder comprehensive in north Warwickshire, in a cup final game at the Barker Butts stadium in Coventry. It was a fine evening towards the end of May. I'd never played on such a splendid pitch. It actually had a covered stand, and the final had attracted 60 or 70 spectators – a crowd, by our standards – comprising parents and teachers. A referee in softly shining maroon livery had been brought in to officiate, and there he was in the centre circle, dispatching a spinning coin into the crisp evening air for the respective captain to make the call.

Win or lose, this would be a great evening. This was it. This was what it was all about. We'd battled through the early rounds, slugging it out deep into the tournament, to emerge victorious from the thrilling scrap of a semi-final that could have gone either way. It was heroic stuff, a schoolboy's dream. No one could spoil our moment.

Well.

I was in my goalmouth limbering up, trying to look the part. I could see that we had won the toss, as our captain had elected that we stay as we were. The referee placed the ball on the centre spot for the kick-off and I started hacking a stud mark in the six-yard line directly in front of the right-hand post, as I always did, for every single game, as a positioning reference. I was about to do the same in front of the left-hand post when I heard a deep-throated cry of umbrage from the touchline.

A cloth-capped guy with the physique of a slug, in those infuriating turned-down wellies, came marching across the pitch towards me. And I mean with that sort of belligerent stride where you get to see the full sole and heel of each oncoming boot before it slaps down hard on the turf. He was purple in the face. There was foam on his lips. He put his mouth about an inch from my face.

'If I see any more of THAT,' he bellowed in the delicate pink conch of my 16-year-old ear, pointing at my stud marks on the freshly painted six-yard line, 'I'll have your guts for GARTERS!'

I was astonished. Laying down a post-marker on the six-yard line was something I'd done for as long as I could remember. It was what the professional goalies did at Coventry City's Highfield Road stadium, home keeper and away. They all did it. At least I *thought* it was what all goalies did.

The markers are incredibly useful. In the thick of the game, you might not think that you even see them, but I knew what all goalies know: the eye at speed processes information that the brain seems not to register. And, what the heck, after 90 minutes the pitch was going to be so pocked with thousands of similar stud marks that it would make no difference. Hell, it wasn't as if they'd have to re-turf the entire pitch just because you'd dragged your stud over an inch or two of the grass near the goalmouth.

I fingered the wax in my ear that the groundsman had just loosened. I looked at the stud marks, then I turned back to him and looked him in the eye.

'Oh, fuck off,' I said, softly.

It was bravado speaking rather than genuine insolence. I'd been so focused on the start of the game that I couldn't believe what he'd just done to upstage the kick-off in front of all those people. And I only said it *very* softly.

He jumped back. I mean he literally and theatrically jumped back the full yard. The next thing I knew, he was calling for the referee.

'Get down here!' he shouted, as if the ref was five years old. 'Get down here now!'

The rest of the boys stood with their hands on their hips as the referee, for some reason, picked up the ball – as if a thief might steal it – and jogged over to us. He was a bald-headed guy with burst veins in his nose, about the same age as the groundsman.

'What's going on?'

'He just told me to fuck off. I want him sent off, no argument.'

The ref looked at me quizzically. I said nothing, so the ref asked me outright if it was true. Instead of answering his question, I said, 'He just walked up to me and screamed right in my ear!' I put a hand over my ear and affected a pained expression. I can do theatre just as well as you, I was telling the groundsman.

The ref looked at old purple face, who in turn pointed an angry finger at the site of my stud marks. 'Look at the state of that! Just look at it!'

By now, we'd been joined by our schoolteacher, Mr Jones, who'd wandered over from the touchline to see what the hell was happening. Jones was a fiery Welsh hardcase and he took no shit. I was terrified that if he was informed that I'd sworn at the groundsman he'd have me off the pitch, military style. I decided to try to get everyone focused on the first offence, not the second. 'I've always done that!' I said, sounding mightily hurt. 'No one has ever told me you can't do that!'

'Do what?' said Jones.

'We break our backs with this pitch,' blustered the groundsman. 'Break our bloody backs. Then these kids come along with no respect for the shop. No respect for the shop at all.'

Jones rubbed his chin judiciously, looked at the stud marks, then at the groundsman. 'It's not a bloody bowling green,' he said.

The groundsman turned to the ref. 'There you are. No respect. None at all. What the hell can you expect when even the teachers are at it?'

Members of my team were by now drifting into the goalmouth to find out what was holding us up.

'Look, he didn't know,' said Jones. 'He knows now, don't you, son?'

I sort of nodded. I looked hurt by it all. Actually, I *was* hurt by it all.

'Can we please get on with the game?' said the ref. 'Please?'

The groundsman seemed to have forgotten the second and more serious offence – the 'fuck off' thing. He was like one of those lumbering rhinos I'd heard about who forget they're chasing you if you hide behind a tree for about three seconds. He wagged an impotent finger in my face before turning and walking off the field, muttering dark oaths. Jones shrugged at me and followed him off. Finally, the game got under way.

We lost that cup final. I was unnerved and didn't play my best game. I'd like to blame it on old purple face, though the truth is we were outplayed. But my grudge against groundsmen, I discover today, seems to have lasted well into its 37th year.

Rhinos: short memories. Goalkeepers: long memories.

Meanwhile, I'm still waiting on this guy to decide whether the game is on. In my mind, it's the same bloke who bellowed at me for marking his pristine six-yard line. He'll love it, making that decision. The power to stop or allow a game of football; it makes his curved little spine tingle, I just know it does.

While we're on the subject, let's examine the business of whether it is actually contrary to the laws of Association football for a goalkeeper to scratch a mark on the pitch. The white lines on the playing field are very clearly designated in the rules and no other markings are allowed, but a stud streak in the mud and a white line are two very different things. When I was a lad, goalies always, always, always dropped a marker at right angles to the goalpost. You never see them do it now because, believe it or not, it can earn you a yellow card. Do it twice and you can actually get sent off for it.

It's just one of the many dirty tricks that Fifa have introduced over the years to make the job of the goalkeeper more difficult: no markers, no back pass to the goalkeeper, the six-second rule; worst of all, stunt balls that swerve as unpredictably as a lurid plastic beach ball on a bracing Skegness beach. Why? So we have more goals. Why do we want more goals in an already perfect game? So that the TV companies can offer more camera excitement and instant replay gratification. Why? So that they can maximise advertising revenue, which will in turn shift more ratburgers and more folding beds. The catering corporations are in league with the purple-faced groundsmen. They're hand-in-glove. Against us.

So, keepers like me now have to resort to limbering up and performing strange exercises at exact right angles to the goalposts, accidentally grazing the grass with our studs to leave guide markers on the six-yard line. I am dedicated to flouting this rule. Passionate about it. I've even thought of carrying (in my little Prada goalie's bag) a small tube of wet unslaked lime to squirt, if I could get away with it. I haven't yet found a way of substituting the stunt balls, but when I do I'll prove that the old, wet, heavy leather lace-up-type balls were much easier to save.

While I've been writing, information has come down the e-tube that the groundsman has made his decision. The grumpy, miserable, puce-faced toerag has called the game *off*, just because he has the power to do so. I can see him now, gritting his tobacco-stained teeth, tugging the peak of his cloth cap and shaking his head. I tell you, I've had it with these groundsmen.

'You must be bloody barmy.'

It's my dad, a retired coal miner, when I tell him that, at the age of 52, I'm going to start playing football again. I add that I've been selected for England. (Oh, all right, England *Writers*, if you insist on edging a story with fine points.)

'What, *you*?' he says. I feel like I'm in one of those

wartime radio monologues about being called upon to form the Home Guard against the imminent Nazi invasion.

'Well, no, not just me. There'll be Phil Oltermann and Patrick Neate ...'

'What, *you*?' say my brothers when I let them in on the story.

'No, there'll be Conrad Williams and Nick Royle and ...'

I mean I really do feel like one of Dad's Army, parading around with a broom handle instead of a genuine rifle, no more a footballer than they were real soldiers. I've got osteoarthritis in the knees, a permanently pulled hamstring and all the visual acuity of a sleeping mole. The sedentary pursuit of a writing career has bequeathed me the reflexes of a sloth bear. The only thing remotely gymnastic-sounding about me is the occasional bout of athlete's foot. I admit that it's all pretty unpromising.

My dad grips the upholstered arm of his chair and chews his cheek, regarding me steadily with rheumy eyes. I point out that Stanley Matthews was still playing top-flight soccer at 50. 'You must be bloody barmy,' he says again.

'*You must be bloody barmy.*' It is the same phrase he threw at me when he came to watch me play for Keresley Newlands primary school. I was 11 years old. Keresley was – pre-Thatcher – a gritty and unlovely coalmining village just north of Coventry. Gritty and unlovely, yes, but bursting with muscular vigour and a menacing sort of pride. In 1966, we had a great team.

That year, we steamrollered pretty much all opposition in the Coventry and District Junior Schools Shield knockout tournament. We progressed through the early rounds with genocidal results. We didn't just beat the opposition, we ate them and burped happily all the way home. With scorelines of 14–0 or 12–1, I'd spend most of the game standing on the edge of my penalty box, jiggling from toe to toe just trying to keep warm. But, of course, the games got progressively harder and soon we would only win by a margin of six or seven goals. As a goalkeeper, I might do nothing all game and still take enormous credit for the strength and success of those burly little miners' sons, righting on the pitch all social injustice and class inequality.

As it became apparent we might go all the way to the final, my dad started coming to watch the games, though he annoyed me by standing behind my goal shouting inappropriate and hopelessly uninformed encouragement. *Swipe it! Leather it! Boot it into touch! Et cetera.* Until in the quarter-final, that is, when he saw me smother the ball by throwing myself at the feet of a breakaway opposition striker. He was appalled. He practically ran onto the pitch and bellowed in my delicate little 11-year-old ear. 'You don't want to do that!' he shouted. 'You'll get your bloody head kicked in!'

There are times in a boy's life when he realises that his dad, who once seemed the oracle of all knowledge, doesn't know the first thing about anything. Anyone who understood football knew that this was part of the job of being a keeper. Going in goal was like signing on for the army: you couldn't later file the complaint that people were shooting bullets at you. This is why, so the cliché goes, all keepers are crazy. To be fair to my dad, goalkeepers of his era had indeed famously been killed and crippled by such heroics.

There's an old joke about goalkeepers. (Actually, it's not a joke at all.) When you are forming an initial assessment of a young goalie, the first thing you ask is this: is he a vampire or is he a crocus? One is afraid of crosses, the other only comes out once a year.

I certainly was never the latter. Goalkeepers learn early that what they lack in skill they can try to make up for with courage. And because I recognised early that my skill level was not of the highest rank, I was always ready to fling myself at the feet of an oncoming striker. Beyond that, and amid all the talk of barmy and crazy, I do often wonder what kink of personality, what twist in the woodgrain it was that made me pull on the green jersey.

The psychology of the goalkeeper is strange. Initially, no one wants the job. When boys gather for a kickaround, it's still usually the runt or the most useless kid who gets shoved between the posts; or the youngest, as a punishment for trailing his elder brother around; or the fat boy, whose corpulence might, for once in his sorry life, be a virtue, in that it obstructs a few extra centimetres of the goal.

So, why would you offer yourself up? Well, there are one or two intelligent forces at work behind this reckless impulse. For one thing, when three dozen kids are swarming like flies round a bull's arse, chasing the ball, you might get only two or three swipes at the leather every half an hour. Go in goal and you will surely enjoy much more of the action. Not so stupid, eh? Not so bad being the fat boy! Not so awful being the youngest! If you've figured that out, it's too late for you. You're on the path. You're now a stick man, confined between the white poles, set apart from the rest and writhing in the net.

You are marked out, even before the first shot of the game, even before you step onto the turf. You sport different colours, thus you are divided even from your own teammates. The rules that apply to them do not apply to you.

As for the others, those who have never pulled on the goalie's jersey, who have never been dedicated to the position themselves, they never know how it feels. No one can make a clown of himself on the pitch like a goalkeeper, because no one else has such spectacular opportunity for error. The worst an outfield player can do is swing his leg at fresh air or fall over his own feet when faced with a gaping goal. These are errors committed often and usually without consequence, but the goalkeeper's mistake very often delivers an easy goal for the opposition.

The catalogue of goalkeeping howlers is endless. There's the fumble, the flap, the punch into the net, the mistimed run, the stranded starfish, the ball through the legs, the bounce over the head . . . The humiliations rack up. And sometimes there are even goals that go in through no fault of our own that still end up making us look like buffoons. I once made a decent save at full stretch to tip a ball onto the bar: it returned off the woodwork, hit me on the back of the head and went in.

Even worse for goalkeepers these days is the technology of multi-angle downloadable media. Though while the YouTube-crazed crowd are shrieking with derision and contempt, and the outfielders are capitalising on the goalie's mortification, you will never find the opposition keeper enjoying the spectacle of another's humiliation. He's been there himself, and often.

At professional level, you will often spot a handshake or an exclusive wink passing between goalies as they change ends or emerge from the tunnel. After the game, there will usually be a consolatory nudge, or even an arm round the shoulder. There is honour between goalkeepers, an unspoken code. A brotherhood. But that special handshake does not represent the self-interest of the Freemason, nor is it about elitism (not when goalies, the cloth-capped proletarians of the game, traditionally command less in the transfer market than all outfielders). It's about empathy. I'm not saying you would die for the other team's goalie – but you often die with him.

It's the summer of 2006 when I get the glorious call-up to play for England. (England? Did I mention that before? Oh, forgive me!) The point is, when the call comes I'm 52 years old and haven't kicked a ball in anger in over 15 years after a cartilage operation on my knee forced me to not only hang up my boots but nail them to a tree. If you know what's good for you, you know when your footballing days are done.

'We hear you're pretty handy between the sticks.' It's Phil Oltermann, a young British writer I've never previously met. I don't know how he's got my name, my number or my utterly obscure footballing history. But I tell him in no uncertain terms I'm not interested in coming out of retirement.

'Sod off.'

'No, I'm serious. We need a goalkeeper.'

'I'm serious, too. Leave me alone.'

'Nigel Spackman says we need you.'

Eh? The only Nigel Spackman I knew was the manager of the then recently relegated League One side Millwall.

'What? The Millwall gaffer?'

'Yes.'

Writers are, of course, capable of outrageous distortion. That's our job, after all, turning out highly embellished stories by the dozen, all based on some barely visible grain of truth. A standard shot becomes a fizzing strike. An ordinary nod of the ball becomes a thumping header. But even given the usual allowances writers make for each other, this was going some. Nigel Spackman didn't know me from an empty pork-scratching packet left under a seat on Row Z.

'See you, Phil!'

The fact of the matter was that Phil had scraped together a Writers' XI to play in – wait for it – the Writers' World Cup to be hosted in Italy in the late summer of that year. Absurdly, the whole competition – flights, hotels in glorious Florence, full kit, and copious wine and beer for an English squad, some unbeatable Swedes, a chain-smoking Hungarian team and, of course, our passionate Italian hosts – is being sponsored by Telecom Italia. It's serious stuff. Well, sort of serious. Half serious. Quarter serious.

Phil had already somehow blagged a coaching session with Spackman at the Millwall training ground, plus a write-up in the press. The luckless Spackman (doomed to be yet another of Millwall's revolving-door managers) must have taken one glance at the bespectacled college types who washed up at the ground because within five minutes he was already arranging for the guy who paints the white lines on the pitch to take over the supervision of this unfeasible crew. In truth, he did cast a jaundiced eye over the fresh-faced scribblers' early exertions.

'Where's your goalkeeper?' Spackman had apparently asked. (I wasn't there at the time.)

'I dare say one of us will go in goal,' Oltermann answered, seriously.

Spackman shook his head. 'No, you need a goalkeeper.'

'Yeah, well, someone will be up for it.'

'Listen to me, you need a goalkeeper.'

Of course, Nigel Spackman didn't specify the recruitment of an obscure genre novelist in his ripe middle age currently living in the East Midlands. But when Oltermann cast wide his net and hauled it in, there just weren't that many green jerseys wriggling inside it. In fact, I think there were only two names that came up, mine being one of them. The other guy couldn't make it to the tournament because he had *some serious thinking to do about things*. Right.

'Look, Phil, my knees are knackered. I wear specs nowadays. I'm out of condition. And I haven't kicked a ball in 20 years.'

'We need you.'

'I'm 52 years old, for God's sake!'

'What, 52? A lovely age for a goalkeeper.'

He asks me to think about it. Trouble is, I can't *stop* thinking about it. I discuss it with my wife, Suzanne, who, of course, still thinks of me as a lithe Adonis, a shot-stopping lycra-clad superhero capable of near-magical feats of agility.

'You bloody idiot!' she replies.

But it's in Florence, I point out to her. And it's all paid for. And Nigel Spackman is correct: mine is, after all, a specialist position.

Building a football team without a goalkeeper is, well, like trying to build a treehouse without a tree, I explain to my wife, whose opinion of the offside law is that it should be scrapped and dumped in the River Soar along with the entire game and all its pundits, fans and attendant media.

I phone Oltermann and tell him I'm in. Then I tell anybody and everybody.

Yeah, England Writers. World Cup. Yeah, Florence. Yeah, World Cup. You didn't know England Writers had a team? Really? Well, not everyone does. Florence, yeah.

Of course, ten minutes after I've agreed to play, I feel a bit bloody stupid. I go and check the web, where there are flashy sites for the various teams. The Italians field semi-pros and produce expensive videos dedicated to their own gorgeousness. The Swedes actually have a former professional, who played for the Swedish national team a few seasons back. I can just see one of his shots 'fizzing' into the back of the net while I've got a finger in my ear rooting around for what I thought was loose wax. The Hungarians don't have an expensive website, but there is a picture of them sporting impressive moustaches and every one of them has a fag on the go.

Off the field, I'm quite relaxed about the prospect of playing again and am looking forward to it greatly. But I know how I am once I'm playing. The instant I'm in a game, every goal that is scored against me I treat as a personal insult. In this I'm sure I'm no different from any other goalkeeper. I don't know why, and I don't care how immature it sounds, but that's how it feels. It doesn't matter whether I pull on the England shirt (tee-hee-hee) or it's coats down for goalposts for a kickaround on the park – each goal conceded is a wound and, let me tell you, no outfielder bleeds like the goalkeeper.

Again, this madness leads me to wonder about the flawed psychology that makes for a keeper. Why go for that least popular and absurdly pressured position? In truth, in those early years no one much wants to be a defender either. The only glory to be had in the kickaround is in the successful strike because that's the place where football detonates. The crowd may rise to its feet at the sight of a thrilling mazy run or a near miss, it may applaud or express dismay or relief at a spectacular goalkeeping save, but there is only one true discharge of tension and that's when the net bulges.

The pleasure of goalkeeping is entirely different. For one thing, it's predicated on everyone else's frustration. Keeping the bastards out is good fun. The hapless kid stuck between the sticks because he's a runt will never appreciate that pleasure, since mostly all he will do is pick the ball out of the net (or, worse, since there isn't usually a net in boys' football, go chasing behind the goal for a ball that either went in or flashed wide, with a depressing sense that he's more ballboy than player). But if you have any flair for the thing, there is huge gratification to be drawn from vexing, exasperating and even maddening the opposition's ambitions.

You very quickly realise there is a craft at stake.

Having agreed to play for this damned silly bloody Writers team, I thought I ought to find out whether I could still kick a ball. I rooted out some kit. My last pair of goalie gloves had rotted at the bottom of a plant pot in the garage. I inspected them ruefully before my dog snatched one out of my hands and buried it at the top of the garden, no doubt with some other decomposing and flavoursome objects. Then, one Sunday afternoon before the approaching tournament, I called on a pal to put me through my paces.

Tanki is a wise and funny brick-built Brummie-Hindu friend who runs the local kids' soccer team. He's a decent back-four stopper himself, but, like many of us, is past his sell-by date in footballing terms. Unlike me, however, he hasn't let himself go to seed. He still looks supple and strong in a pair of shorts and boots. In fact, my old boots, when I unearthed them and a colony of wood spiders from behind the gas meter in the cupboard under the stairs, seemed to have spawned mildew and blue-green algae, and to have cultivated a mysterious cotton-like white fungus that was sprouting from the lace-holes.

Anyway, Tanki kindly agreed to come over to the local park with me. The brief was to try to get me back in shape. He'd brought half a dozen balls with him in a net. Very official. He fired in a few shots and we did a bit of intense close work. We did shot–recover–shot–recover, using his lad as a protesting ballboy. Some of my goalkeeping skills came back immediately, but if you don't have certain goalkeeping skills in the first place, they can't come back, can they? What was shocking was how quickly I remembered how crap I was.

'Let's be honest,' Tanki said gently after half an hour, in a way that made me afraid of this honesty. 'Your handling is OK, but you're not fit.'

I'm not sure what prompted him to make this remark. It may have been the shiny aubergine hue that had developed on my face in that hardly strenuous half-hour, or the industrial proportions of sweat-salt crusting visibly on my corrugated brow. Or just that I was lying face down on the floor, refusing to get up.

When I called it a day, he said, still mindful of the need

for honesty, 'Let's be truthful here, Graham: what are you worried about anyway?'

'Worry? Me, worry? Well, OK. I haven't played in nearly 20 years, that's what. I don't want to look like a fool.'

Tanki chewed a blade of grass, ruminatively, as they say, looking at me like there was nothing to be done to prevent this particular scenario, and nor had there ever been.

'Plus,' I said, 'I don't want to let anyone down.'

He sat on the grass, cross-legged like Gandhi – well, not quite like Gandhi, since Tanki wasn't particularly partial to sitting in the park in a loincloth – and treated me to a bit of homespun Brummie-Hindu wisdom. 'Truthfully, Graham, what do they expect? You're an old fuck like me.'

'Thanks, Tanki. Is that what they call blue-sky thinking? You should go into business as a life motivator.'

'Look, mate, you do your best and if anyone is going to feel let down, they can fuck off.'

Right. Glad we got that cleared up. That's squared me up nicely for the tournament.

As it happened, I wasn't to get sight of my England Writers' XI teammates until I joined them at Heathrow on the plane for Florence. Delays on the road and because of the interminable security measures that are the misery of modern airports meant that the rest of the squad were in their cabin seats well before I was able to slide my flight bag into the overhead locker. Apparently, there had been some anxiety about whether I might turn up at all.

I did know two members of the squad: Nick Royle and Conrad Williams, both very fine horror writers who I was hoping would line up in front of me, but they were flying in from Manchester – which is the sort of place you'd expect horror writers to be from.

Seems right, doesn't it? Four gargoyle-like horror novelists in the back line, a couple of the more fancy literary-type scribblers performing elegant footwork on the flanks, a brace of solid award-winning authors doing fashionable stuff no one understands in midfield and a thriller writer up front. This was to be the nearest we got to tactical play.

I was still glancing up and down the plane for what might look like the usual characteristics of a football team – chiselled jaws; vacant, fish-eyed expressions; the shiftiness of a casual rapist, all that – when my elbow was jogged by a couple of college boys. Phil Oltermann, the principal architect of this madcap adventure, and Matt Weiland, deputy editor at the time of the highly regarded by ponces *Granta* magazine, turned out to be more than competent footballers, but at that moment I was slightly nonplussed. Phil – tall, reed-thin and rather gangly – is a handsome fellow behind his spectacles. Likewise Matt, with a diminutive frame that belies his physical strength. They both swear they weren't, but somehow my memory of that moment has them wreathed in Oxford scarves. They were very charming; they just looked like they'd turned up for a seminar on medieval poetry and a little like you might be able to blow them off their stalks like seed dandelions.

After shaking hands with what approached reasonable firmness for Oxbridge types, they re-took their seats next to a guy who looked like the drummer in a rock band. A '70s rock band, reformed after all the booze and drugs and rehabilitation and – who'd have thought it! – out on the road after all these years. He wore a broad-rimmed Jimi Hendrix black fedora and sported massive silver rings on every finger. Jed Novick was a biographer, I was told, of Benny Hill.

Fucking 'ell, I thought. College boys and rock veteran experts on Benny Hill. And me in goal, pretending I know what I'm doing. This should be good.

I do have a theoretical knowledge of the job in hand; I mean I know where to stand. And, no, it's not in the bloody middle of the goal.

My uncle Harold winked at me and pointed at the Coventry City goalkeeper Bill Glazier. It was 1964, the season that Jimmy Hill guided the club to promotion from Division Three. Uncle Harold, a puckish, grey-haired, pipe-smoking man, with a permanent twinkle in his eye, introduced me to the football terraces of old. He would carry a small stool to the ground for me to stand on in his favoured position: behind and just to the left of the goal about seven rows back on the old Spion Kop. In those days, football grounds smelled of three things: meat pies, the printer's ink that came off the football programme onto your fingers, and pipe tobacco.

Uncle Harold bit on the stem of his rosewood pipe and smiled at me. 'Knows where to stand,' he said. 'That's why he cost so much money.'

I must have looked puzzled because Uncle Harold went on to explain how Bill Glazier covered his angles.

Glazier had been signed by Jimmy Hill for what was then a world record fee for a goalkeeper of £35,000. There's no way today a third-flight club has a few million to spare to break any kind of record transfer. Jimmy Hill may seem a bit of a pillock in the eyes of many, but he had the sense to recognise the value of a great goalkeeper. I studied Glazier that day. I can't recall who Coventry were playing that afternoon, but I do remember the pungent scent of Briar pipe tobacco and that nothing got past Glazier. Angles; I felt that my uncle Harold had disclosed to me not only one of the great secrets of goalkeeping but also one of the great secrets of life.

Even today I'm sure that many football aficionados fail to grasp that the highest technical accomplishment in the craft of goalkeeping is knowing where to stand. In fact, it behoves all footballers to spend some time goalkeeping so that they might get the magical insight. What the goalkeeper knows is that although where he stands might not necessarily mean that he can make the save, it will certainly increase the chances of making the striker miss.

Football commentators on the telly are routinely too bloody thick to appreciate this. They will often commend a great save by the goalkeeper, but I've never once heard a pundit on TV or radio recognise that a striker's shot was off target because of where the goalkeeper was standing. 'Should have been on target,' they'll say, shaking their heads. Why, when to have been on target would have slotted it straight down the goalkeeper's throat? Surely flashing the shot just wide of the upright was of equal value when there was no other option? 'Should have done better. Should have been on target.' The orange facepaint they have to wear in the TV studios must seep into their blood and muddy their brains.

When a keeper is perfectly positioned against an angled shot, unless it's a perfect strike it's not going anywhere except into the keeper's midriff or wide of the post. Under pressure, the striker has a split fraction of a second to place his shot and the goalkeeper's position alone can distract him enough to do the defensive job. The keeper has 'saved' a goal without even touching the ball, or maybe even without moving a muscle.

'Should have been on target.' Meh.

Of all the goalkeeper's attributes, positioning is king. It comes ahead of the other essential attributes of handling, shot-stopping, speed out of goal, courage in the one-on-one, aerial command and confident body language. Non-goalkeepers often fail to understand that the art of goalkeeping is as much about making the striker miss as it is about stopping shots; it's as much about putting the striker under pressure as it is about flinging your body across the face of the goal. Goalkeeping operates on the happy negative more than it does on the positive. It sounds odd, but more misses – I mean shots off target – can be put down to good goalkeeping than they can to bad striking.

I'll hold up my hands and admit I'm a lousy goalkeeper. I shouldn't even be allowed on the pitch. But I do know where to stand.

My boyhood hero, and probably England's finest goalkeeper, was Gordon Banks. What a funny-looking guy. His appearance certainly belied the athlete he really was. A former coal merchant, he had a slight stoop and no neck, which made it look like he was always tucking his chin into his shoulder against the pressure of the half-hundredweight sacks he used to deliver from the back of a coal lorry. And he had a squint, even before the accident in which he lost the sight in one eye. Oh, and he also had a terrible case of goalkeeper's traditional bad haircut, but we won't go into that.

Banks was a goalkeeping genius. His ratio of goals conceded to international games played is incredible. In his seventy-three international appearances, England lost only nine games. Nine! (And take it from someone who was there, even when we won the World Cup we were never as superior as the result suggests.) He kept 35 clean sheets and his average concession of goals per game was 0.78.

His absence (through food poisoning) during the 1970 World Cup quarter-finals is commonly held to be the reason for England's defeat by West Germany. At the time of the tournament in Mexico, there were two players in the England team who were seen as capable of neutralising the great Pele. Those two were Gordon Banks and Bobby Moore. Before the competition had even begun, Moore was badly unsettled after being arrested, though never charged, for allegedly stealing a bracelet from a jeweller's shop in Colombia. Banks was then mysteriously struck by food poisoning, while the rest of the team remained unaffected, even though their diet was regulated. Conspiracy theories were dismissed as 'wild'. The suggestion that the England team had been got at was dismissed – at the time – as ridiculous. The idea that South American gambling cartels and drug-barons – gangsters not above shooting dead a footballer if, say, he happened to accidentally score an own goal – might for betting purposes conspire to influence the outcome of the World Cup is obviously an outrageous slur on murderous South American gangsters everywhere.

There were many goalkeepers more spectacular than Banks. Peter 'the Cat' Bonetti was a fantastically agile keeper regularly given to acrobatic leaps and handsome gymnastic springs. (He was substituted for Banks for the 1970 quarter-final, but a couple of keeper errors ended England's claim to the title.) Banks was never a goalkeeper given to histrionics and full-length dives. His 'save of the century', a diving save against Brazil, which Pele himself described as the finest stop he had ever seen – a powerful downward header from the Emperor of All Football Everywhere just inside the upright was somehow flipped over the crossbar – was all the more remarkable because of some uncanny positioning that enabled Banks to get to a ball to which he had no earthly right. Banks knew where to stand.

He exemplified the principle of Right Position, which is itself based on anticipation. Old footage of Banks reveals a constant sideways creeping, a sequence of minor crab-like adjustments, even when there is no apparent threat. Then when the real danger manifested itself, the footwork of this former coal merchant would outshine Nijinsky – the Russian ballet dancer, not the bloody winner of the Epsom Derby and the Two Thousand Guineas. Yet he was the exact opposite of a showman.

Banks's no-nonsense style of goalkeeping proceeded from the single principle that if you're standing in the right place when the strike is made, you won't need to fling yourself across the face of the goal. He threw himself about less than other keepers because he didn't need to. The records speak for themselves.

And another thing about Gordon Banks: he knew where a shot was going before it had even left a striker's foot. Banks was an intuitive. It's not a magical act; it is pure athleticism and speed of hand–eye coordination. The eye of a highly attuned athlete reads information and processes it in a way that bypasses the brain. The report goes direct to muscle, to reflex. Banks, and many great goalkeepers, read the body language of the opposition striker and this, coupled with his experience of the game, told him where the ball was going to go before it was struck.

All this in the 1960s and early '70s, when there was barely any specialised goalkeeper training or coaching.

Two years later, Banks's goalkeeping supremacy was over. Returning from Stoke City's Victoria Ground on a Sunday after physio treatment following a 2–1 defeat at Liverpool the day before, his Ford Granada collided with a van. He lost the sight in one eye. He could still play but never to the same fabulous high standards. He then went to the US to play for Fort Lauderdale Strikers in the North American Soccer League, where he earned a certain ignominious fame as a one-eyed goalkeeper.

Ol' one eye. I know it sounds like I'm making this up as I go along, but I'm not.

It's difficult to imagine how carrying coal from the back of a lorry shaped his goalkeeping prowess, but he had the total package. As a lad, I wanted to be like Gordon Banks. I used to try to copy his movements. He used to stand like a monkey in goal. That's about as far as I got in emulation. In fact, I was kind of the opposite of Banks. Even if a shot came straight at me, I'd grab it, pause for a moment, then fling myself full stretch, left or right, as a kind of spectacular afterthought, a bit of heroic punctuation. After all, you don't know who might be watching.

There's one other detail that links me to Gordon

Banks. When he was a young player, he was sent packing by Romarsh Welfare FC of the Yorkshire League after only two games with the club. In those two games, he'd managed to let in fifteen goals! I must have managed that, but late rather than early in my footballing career; in fact, in my current England set-up, with the Writers' team, who are all fucking useless, every one of them. Still, when the team in front of you are a bunch of deadbeats, you get to fling yourself about a bit.

I probably honed the skill of unnecessary spectacular diving when playing for my primary-school team. As I said, I would often only be called upon once or twice in a game to make any kind of save. Consequently, I was always determined to milk it. I could never bear the idea of going home with a clean goalkeeper's shirt. Even a stately back pass from one of my own teammates (you could pick the ball up in those days) would be an excuse for flinging myself in the mud. It was like I practised goalkeeping by wrestling with a cardboard box. Really, I should have gone into the theatre. But, you know, coalmining background and all that. Even if you genuinely did like 1950s musicals, you're not going to tell anyone, are you?

Mr Ship, the schoolteacher who organised our pit-village primary-school team, called all the hopefuls into the classroom at lunchtime and picked the team by throwing shirts at you. He had a big leather bag of shirts. What working-class people used to call a hold-all. The first shirt out of the hold-all he chucked at the centre-half.

'Captain,' he said. The next one at the centre-forward. 'Up front.' Oh, the brief flight of those shirts through the pregnant classroom air. The third one he chucked at me. I caught it. 'In goal.'

He played out this ritual every Friday lunchtime (*dinnertime, dinnertime*, we called the midday break *dinnertime*) before a Saturday game. He did change the team occasionally, so although you felt reasonably secure you were always reminded that other lads were waiting, breathless, big-eyed, hoping to take your place. But he always started with the old-fashioned spine of the team. Tough centre-half. Aggressive centre-forward. Goalkeeper. Then he proceeded to nominate around that spine. If I were to pick a team today, despite the pundits' system variations and the tactical notions that swirl fraudulently around my head, I'd probably do the very same thing: fix the spine first.

We continued to flatten most of the opposition with those scores of 9–1, 11–0 or 7–1. Another pipe-sucking uncle regularly raised one eyebrow and asked me if we'd been playing the School for the Blind. 'That's not politically correct, Uncle Jim,' I might not have responded every single week he said it, but, even as team goalkeeper, it was possible for me to play without touching the ball for the entire game and still garner great personal kudos from these sweeping victories. I don't know why we used to win by such margins; perhaps our mining-village team was a bit beefier in a way that intimidated a lot of 11 year olds, but these are the facts.

At that time, the Coventry education authorities ran a primary schools' challenge shield tournament and, after our school retained the trophy for the seventh consecutive year, Keresley Newlands primary school was ruled ineligible for all subsequent years that the competition was staged. The reason cited was that a minor boundary change had occurred. We know otherwise. What had unlovely Keresley pit-village got to shout about? A shitty, crumbling youth club; a dilapidated library with peeling paint that opened two evenings a week; a primary-school tradition of stomping all-comers at football. This last they took away. Get used to it, someone might have said, because in a few years they'll take away the pit, too, and all that goes with it.

Nevertheless, it was in this context that we progressed to the quarter-finals of the above competition and were scheduled to face, away from home on a fine spring evening after classes, a school with the fabulously exotic name of Our Lady of the Assumption.

'Catholics,' said Keith Randle, our beatific and unstoppable centre-forward, a lad permanently given to flicking a fringe of golden hair out of his blue eyes. 'Left-footers.'

I thought for a while about the footballing implications of this.

We changed in the same shower room as the opposition, eyeing each other furtively; little lads slapping muscle rub on their chubby thighs in imitation of the pros. The air was charged with Sloan's Liniment and high expectation. They looked a tall, gangly crew, and a lot of them seemed to have excessive overbites, which rather perversely I thought might have something to do with their Catholicism. Then their captain, a well-spoken lad, came across and asked us to identify our 'skipper'. We pointed to Mick Carpenter, centre-half, captain by dint of being team hard case.

'Welcome to Our Lady.' The boy offered a hand that

wanted shaking. 'Here's to a good game, and may the best side win.'

Mick Carpenter, a strong, silent type, stared at him with cloudless, unblinking eyes. We were all arrested in the act of pulling on shirts and tying bootlaces. For a moment, it seemed as if Mick was going to reject the outstretched hand, but finally he offered his own, staring the boy down and solemnly shaking hands without saying a word. The boy coloured and went back to his cohorts. Mick Carpenter glanced round at the rest of us. I must admit we had little time for all that sporting shit; we just wanted to crunch people 10–0.

The game was an unexpected struggle. By half-time, we were leading 2–1 and, in the shock of having to do something, I was playing out of my skin. What I lacked in skill, I tried to make up for by being prepared to fling myself gymnastically at anyone's feet, whatever the risk, and this I did that evening. I tipped one shot over the bar, palmed another round the post, got my body behind a stinging close-range effort. It was my best game to date. I was pressed into service again and again. None of us were used to this. It was a real game of football. They were matching us blow for blow.

A short time into the second half, they pulled level, and after that they turned the screw. They were set to give us a pasting and suddenly my team, who so confidently travelled around Coventry steamrollering all opposition, looked like frightened little boys. We somehow hung on until the final whistle blew and we changed round immediately for a bout of extra time.

Back they came at us. Every single body was clustered in our own penalty area and we spent 15 minutes frantically scrambling, scooping, heading and clearing balls off the line. Shot after shot. Outrageously, the home referee-teacher, anxious to see his boys press the advantage, allowed the game to run on five or six minutes after the second bout of extra time. Mr Ship was furiously trying to call time from the touchline, to no avail. He was angry in a way we'd never seen before. Then came the opposing captain – the sporting handshake kid – shining with a kind of last-gasp ardour, stepping round every lunging tackle we could offer, until he was through, with only me to beat. I'd had the goalkeeping game of my young life that day and I wasn't going to let him score.

So, I poleaxed him. By which I mean I flung myself at his feet with a limited expectation of getting the ball but knowing that, whether I got the ball or not, he would topple.

The boy went down with a groan. I gathered the loose ball and gave it the old-fashioned bounce-bounce-boot, as if everything was normal. The referee stood inches away, looking deep into my eyes. He was agonising over his decision, the silver whistle glinting and trembling between his lips.

The referee understood perfectly that he'd shamefully abused his authority, that he'd stepped beyond the bounds of all sporting decency by ignoring the clock. He had disgracefully favoured his own lads to the point where he could barely live with himself. Precisely because of all that, he was in no position to award what, under any other conditions, would have been a clear penalty.

He had one last opportunity to vouchsafe a sliver of his tattered integrity. He blew the whistle, not for a penalty, but for full-time. A replay would be necessary.

Now's the time to deal with that tiresome Albert Camus thing that gets quoted everywhere, that everything he knew about morality in life he'd learned from football. OK, in this case he knew what he was talking about.

We won the replay 4–2 and went on to win the Coventry Shield.

That was a day on which I'd just decided to make my presence felt. Positioning and anticipation are two of the less obvious attributes of a good goalkeeper (well, less obvious than shot-stopping and catching the ball), but there are more. Presence is another crucial, but more elusive, factor in goalkeeping.

'The custodian,' it says in the nineteenth-century pamphlet *Preparations for Footballing*, 'must be a stout and redoubtable fellow with the presence to command his line.' How they loved that word *custodian*, with its formal implications of guardian, curator, prison warder even. I quite like it, too. I've been going around using it for a few days now.

So, the custodian must have the capacity to dominate the goal area or, more particularly, the area between the penalty spot and the goal. He requires the ability to inspire confidence in the defenders and scare up some dismay in the opposition attack line. Presence is established in many ways; the skill to deal confidently with crosses, whether by catch or punch, is, of course, essential. But there's much more to it than that. Often it's about making yourself big in front of an oncoming striker and not going to ground too early in order to encourage them to miss the target. Further it involves organising defenders around you in order to reduce the number of times your goalkeeping skills are actually pressed into service.

Just as with the matter of standing in the right position, a great deal of goalkeeping is about dominating the action in such a way that your shot-stopping abilities are never actually called into question.

My own candidate for the Greatest Ever Goalkeeper of All Time would be Peter Schmeichel, a player in possession of the full set of goalkeeping skills, and perhaps the one most equipped with the attribute of commanding presence. Off the field, he appears to be the most mild-mannered of men – a gentle giant – but to see him bellowing at his Manchester United back line was a joy. He was like a fishwife berating a wayward husband at the door of the alehouse. What a gob he had on him! When he had something to say, his jaw came down to his knees. He seemed to regard it as a personal betrayal if ever an attacker was allowed to get in a strike unchallenged; if ever a shot came his way, someone in a red shirt in front of him wasn't doing their job. Why should I clean up where your poodle pissed, he seemed to be shouting. Loudly and often.

He probably changed the character of modern British goalkeeping, too. Before Schmeichel, the leaden wisdom was the orthodoxy of the clean catch. As a boy, it was drummed into me that the goalie shalt catch not parry a shot, and take not punch a cross. It's pretty obvious why this became the approved lesson. The clean catch stops the game, gives your defence a chance to regroup and puts possession back on your side.

David James, a superb keeper despite some much-publicised errors, says he was drilled in this virtue over and over as a young player. It's probably this background of drilling that has made a vampire out of James. The game has changed. Gone are the days of the predictable cross, lobbed at the far post – the easiest for the keeper to pluck out of the air. Not only has the game changed, so has the laminate and stitching of the ball. It was far easier to take a heavier ball on a clear trajectory than the spinning, dipping, lightweight, modern stunt version we play with nowadays. I think these changes have played havoc with James's confidence with the cross. I'm not excusing the flapping, but a goalkeeper drilled to a bygone era and as a result riddled with fear is of no use to anyone. Just get out there and punch the bloody thing, and reconfigure your defence to expect that.

When I was a schoolboy, punching the cross was seen as some weird, foreign aberration. It was unmanly and Italian, akin to that creepy habit some Mediterranean chaps have of carrying a small leather handbag. Ditto parrying or otherwise failing to catch a shot cleanly. But Schmeichel came along and taught us that there is only one true gospel of the gloves: keep the ball out of the net, by all means possible.

Schmeichel would punch if he was at all uncertain about a catch, and what a punch. He would parry a hard drive, and if a shot was fired in on the rebound he would parry that, too. He might save with his knee, or his foot, or his elbow, or with his big Danish bollocks, if necessary. It didn't matter. His agility was a sensation. He developed a curious star jump to block the close shot or the one-on-one (supposedly traced back to some ice hockey goalkeeping from his younger days). It all went completely against the drill. It went against stuff every young goalkeeper in England had been brainwashed with for decades. Several pundits monitoring his strange style of goalkeeping seriously doubted Alex Ferguson's wisdom in signing the Dane for Manchester United.

Pundits, eh, Sir Alex?

Schmeichel was utterly in command of his area. He made the goal look small. He terrorised his back four into constantly pressuring the opposition. He launched attacks from the back line. He was a charismatic powerhouse. Young goalkeepers can't dominate those older, more experienced players in front of them, which is why at the time of writing Ben Foster, Scott Carson, Chris Kirkland and the top-drawer Robert Green can be factored out of the reckoning for the England number 1 shirt in games other than friendlies. Their time will come, but it isn't now.

And also, at the time of writing, over a dozen of the 20 Premiership clubs favour a non-English keeper, as do all of the high-spending big four. Could it be that our crusty old coaches are still training our young goalkeepers in the wrong principles?

Another great keeper in the mould of Schmeichel is Oliver Kahn. Kahn has lived up to the keeper-craziness cliché at times, but his work ethic has earned him fierce respect. His handling is as reliable as anyone's, but he often prefers to punch any questionable cross or shot rather than make a potentially risky attempt to hold the ball. It's a safety-first principle at the highest level.

Admittedly, he is a nutcase, too. A national hero in Germany, he did what any goalie does from time to time: he made an error. OK, this one happened to be crucial in the 2002 World Cup final. Shame, that. He fumbled a shot and gifted a goal to Brazil's Ronaldo. His face was *Oh, bugger*. Despite this, he was deservedly awarded Player of the Tournament. And despite *that*, he went on

German TV and wept. Yes, wept and shook with remorse over the goal that lost Germany the final. You do want to say, hang on a bit . . . But here's an interesting footnote: a subsequent survey showed that 90 per cent of German males thought he was a bloody silly ninny (that's a loose translation) for crying on prime-time TV, *whereas* 90 per cent of German women indicated that they would very much like to have his babies. Hmm.

Not that I would ever cry about it, and not that anyone, least of all a prime-time TV audience, would notice if I did, but that anxiety about letting your teammates down (or an entire country's footballing aspirations, if you happen to be an international keeper, like Kahn) through making a goalkeeping howler is always there, the long-tongued leering demon just above your shoulder, perched on the crossbar, waiting to gnaw on your liver.

'WD-40.'

'You what?'

'WD-40.'

'What?'

It's my dad again, dispensing sports medicine from his armchair. I've been moaning about the osteoarthritis in my knee and fretting about how my ligaments are going to hold up for the tournament. My knees are knackered; too much football over the years, plus a fair bit of aggressive downhill skiing, has ruined the cartilage in both my knees. I had a succesful arthroscopy on one knee several years ago, but the operation often creates problems of osteoarthritis later on in life, and so the problems came back. Where the cartilage is worn away, the bones grind together. It's worse in cold weather, and under stress it can be pretty painful. My dad is extolling his latest remedy. 'You bloody heard me. WD-40. Get some of that on it.'

WD-40 is an all-purpose mechanical lubricant. You can spray it on your car engine if it's damp. You can spray it on your bike chain if it's a bit rusty. In fact, if it's damp, jammed, rusted, seized, squeaking or just plain dirty, you put some of this stuff on it, whistle cheerfully for a few seconds, wipe your hands on a dirty rag and it's all fixed. Actually, if you were able to massively overcharge yourself for the job, you could walk away feeling like a proper qualified mechanic.

You just don't put it on your fucking knees, and I said so.

'There you are,' he said. 'You know nothing. You've got all your degrees and books published and doctorates and muffins [*muffins? I don't know anything about muffins and have no idea what he meant*] and still you know nothing and you're too bloody big-headed to learn about anything.'

This is an old tune. I think it started when I was 11. Even though I failed my eleven-plus exams, I went off to a 'posh comprehensive' (i.e. slightly lower underage pregnancy and crime rates among the schoolchildren than the nearby secondary modern) and came back too big-headed to know anything about anything. College massively exacerbated this big-headed condition. A writing career put me beyond the pale.

'It's a bloody mechanical spray!' I protested. 'What are you talking about?'

'Let me tell *you*,' he said, jabbing a finger at *me*, 'that it was developed for space-flight technology and ...'

'I don't know about that.'

'Shut up, big-'ead. It was developed for space-flight technology and people have used it for all sorts, including joints inflammation and ...'

'Well, I'm not bloody well using it.'

'Well, if you're too big-headed ...' Etc., etc.

The thing about my old man is he's a passionate improviser. If Dad ever took a minor injury while working down the pit, he would prefer to make do rather than come to the surface for treatment (because you lost a day's pay if you clocked off early, and that *was* a serious matter), so he got in the habit of carrying a tube of superglue with him at work, smearing any cut or gaping wound that might need a stitch with the ol' super-bonder. Anyway, one day after he'd retired he was doing a bit of DIY around the house when he gashed his finger. It needed a stitch or two, but, as I say, Chairman Bill is not one to clutter up the Accident and Emergency unit at the local hospital. No fear, out with the superglue!

Now, I don't know about you, but I always find superglue to be completely crap unless you want to bond your own skin, in which case it works with the Devil's might. And on this occasion, when he accidentally touched his thumb to the finger wound, thumb and forefinger of right hand became passionately conjoined. Drat, he thinks, but no worries: a bit of spit will sort that out. His first spit missed the mark, so for accuracy he lifted his commingled digits to his mouth. And touched his lip.

So, now he's got finger and thumb wedded to his bottom lip. Yet what makes him really cross is the fact that

I happen to walk into the house to find him with head under the cold faucet, trying to sluice the superglue away.

'Shay bloody noshing,' he mumbles at me, 'or you're dead.'

So, although he may be right about the WD-40, I tend to resist buying into his patent remedies, snake oils and spray-can solutions for osteoarthritic footballers. Call me a wuss.

Though I must admit, what with the tournament in Italy looming, I did think about it. In fact, I went and had a poke about in the garage to find the can of WD-40. I sprayed a bit on the back of my hand just to check it didn't actually peel off layers of skin and leave me looking like one of those purple walking corpses from *Night of the Living Dead*. I also gave it a sniff, for good measure.

All right, I thought, can't hurt to give it a try. I unbuckled my belt and dropped my trousers. I was just about to spray my knees with the stuff when the garage door flew open. Instinctively, I grabbed the handle and slammed the door shut.

'What are you doing in there?' It was my wife, Suzanne.

'Just a minute.'

I let go of the door handle, so I could pull up my pants.

The door flew open again. 'What are you up to?'

I stood there, with my trousers round my knees, gripping the can of WD-40. I couldn't have felt more embarrassed, or looked more shifty, if she'd caught me clutching a copy of *Readers' Wives*.

'WD-40,' I said vaguely. I advertised the can to her, for confirmation.

'What?'

'WD-40. Just spraying it on my knees.'

'What?!'

It seemed to me that I'd just made up the wackiest ever excuse that a man might offer his wife for being caught with his trousers down. Even I didn't believe it. And because I didn't believe it myself, I gave both knees a thorough dousing, just to prove to us both that it might be true.

'You're insane! What the heck are you doing?'

'Aerospace research. Joints. That sort of thing.'

I think she believed me, ultimately. Possibly. As for the experiment, did it help? Well, *you betcha*, as they say in Upper Killay. The old bones were actually lubricated by the stuff and, though it did turn my knees an alarming, shiny fire-engine red, I resolved to pack a can in my goalie's bag for export to Italy.

Ahem.

Really, it's an extraordinary thing to want to do, to be a goalkeeper. When the aim of the team and the ardent desire of the spectator is to engineer or see engineered the heart-stopping electric flashpoint and the delirious thrill of a goal going in for your side, the goalkeeper is the wet blanket, the killjoy, the party pooper. He's the dog at the gate, the miserly dragon at the mouth of the cave of treasures.

Rule 4 of the laws of the game clearly states that 'each goalkeeper wears colours which distinguish him from the other players, the referee and the assistant referees'. The goalkeeper's objective is distinct from all the other players' ambitions and his outside status is advertised in fancy garb. For a long time, the conventional goalie's colour was green, with yellow as reserve. There was always a bit of variation over the years, but you would need a sociologist to say why in the mid-1990s the design of goalies' shirts went haywire. Both at club and international level, keepers started to appear in shitty psychedelic sweaters that looked like they'd been designed by a depressed LSD casualty funded by an arts council grant. Must have been millennium fever. The designs did recover and are now pretty sober again; even green has started to make a comeback.

Yet even though he has to tog up like the motley fool, it is the goalkeeper alone who connects furthest back with the traditions and history of the game. Only the goalkeeper carries the true bloodline of the sport, because only he plays the kind of football from which the game so recently evolved. Yes, everyone else on the park is a parvenu, an upstart. The goalkeeper alone can boast patrician blood.

Though if we have to drag class into it, football was not always the working-class sport it is now (or was, until the advent of what Roy Keane angrily dubbed the 'prawn-sandwich brigade'). About 150 years ago, an important meeting took place at Cambridge University of representatives of several public schools: Harrow, Eton, Westminster, Marlborough and a few others. Basically, every toffs' academy you justifiably hate. The Victorian schools were very keen indeed on strenuous physical activity for the lads, and with one very good reason: they saw it as an antidote to some of the 'beastly' activities posh teenage boys are prone to get up to in the dorm after lights out, the sort of stuff that might get you expelled from Eton but some like to call networking at another public school which must remain unnamed. There are a lot of people at the BBC and in the Foreign Office who know exactly what I'm talking about.

Having the boys run up and down a muddy field three times a week was seen as a healthy, energy-sapping alternative to all this dorm-time depravity and beastliness, and schools became very interested in challenging each other to games. But there was a problem: massive variation in the rules of the game. At that time, playing football was not unlike going into a pub in Manchester today to shoot a few frames of pool. Some local lout will always come up with a dubious regional variation of the rules designed to ensure that you lose. Anyway, the above meeting laid down the very first of what was to be a succession of Cambridge Rules: a formula under which all players in a ten-men-per-side game were allowed to catch the ball directly from the foot, provided they kicked it on immediately. Catching it and kicking it, rather like a modern goalkeeper does today, was allowed. Running with the ball, though, was against the rules.

About a decade later, former pupils of the more rugged Sheffield Collegiate School established the Sheffield Football Club at Bramall Lane. Wanting to put a bit of steel back into the game, in 1857 they published their own set of rules for football, allowing for more physical contact than those rules established by the Cambridge cissies. Players were allowed to push opponents off the ball with their hands. It was also within the rules to shoulder charge opposition players, with or without the ball, in the style of modern American football, but presumably without the girly suits of armour worn on the other side of the Atlantic. Under these rules, a player catching the ball might concede a goal by being barged over the line. Even to this day, you hear old lags at a game, sucking mints and going, 'blah, blah, Nat Lofthouse', lamenting the passing of the days when burly centre-forwards were allowed to commit aerial GBH on the goalkeeper with the intention of bundling both over the goal-line.

When the Football Association was set up in 1863, its initial aim was to settle a unifying code for the game. The first secretary was Ebenezer Cobb Morley (again, I swear I'm not making all this up), a man made of sterner mettle than the present incumbents, for it was his job to crack heads and amalgamate the rules observed by the public schools and the football clubs. If only social division could be bridged so easily today, for the glorious Ebenezer emerged with a set of 23 rules. (The famous William Webb Ellis story about the founding of rugby football is a complete load of cock – rugby emerged after an angry schism and a failure of certain football clubs to agree to this new code. One of the sticking points was the business of hacking, i.e. chopping your opponent anywhere from the waist down. The schism hardened and the more conservative form of the game was maintained in rugby football, itself to evolve later.) Things kept changing, and in 1870 ten-a-side games were extended by the addition of a goalkeeper, hence the mysterious and irregular number of eleven players that now comprise a team.

The goalkeeper is the 11th man.

An 1867 update dictated: 'A goal shall be won when the ball passes between the goalposts under the tape, not being thrown, knocked on, or carried.' The new rules distinguished between goalkeepers and other players for the very first time: 'A player shall not throw the ball nor pass it to another, except in the case of the goalkeeper, who shall be allowed to use his hands for the protection of his goal . . . No player shall carry or knock on the ball; nor shall any player handle the ball under any pretence whatever.' The old handling game was over, except, of course, in the case of the goalkeeper. It is ironic that it was only the additional player, the 11th man, who connected back to the old rules.

Note the reference to tape: crossbars became compulsory after goalkeepers started pulling on the tape so that a shot might sail right over it. As goalkeeping technique goes, it beats getting your shirt dirty. I must admit it would drive you crackers if you were a striker, but I do warm to the idea of a keeper tugging down the tape and winking provocatively at someone with the temperament of Wayne Rooney after he's just blasted over.

Anyway, after crossbars were introduced, nets came along in 1892 to end all disputes because, football being football, everyone is a cheat at some point.

What with the hostility and proximity of the crowds, you wouldn't much want to be a fat boy in goal. Today, that's often where the fat boy still gets shoved. Though I myself can modestly profess to sporting a more athletic shape, there's good reason why you fat chaps might find yourselves located between the sticks. Here's a message of hope and cheer for the fat boys amongst us: yours is a rightful position, with a strong clear heritage, so next time they sing about the pies, wear your fat with pride.

And your cap. Though it has spun right out of fashion, most pre-war photographs show the keeper sporting a cloth cap. (Why do they always say 'sporting' when it comes to headgear, even if the bloke in question is doing nothing more athletic than shuffling down the Queen's Arms to get himself a pie and a pint?) Occasionally, these days, you might see a keeper put on a silk jockey-style cap to keep the sun out of his eyes, but most keepers in the old photos are playing in the gloomy depths of an English winter under a blanket of traditional industrial smog.

More history lessons for the fat boy at the back of the class: remember, at that time all players could catch the ball and kick it on, and it was quite within the rules to shoulder charge opponents. You could muscle them out of the way whether they had the ball or not; you just gave them a good bruising. If a player was caught napping with the ball, he could be barged over the line. What larks!

Then came the 1872 update to the code laid down by the Sheffield Collegiate School, dictating that only the goalkeeper could handle the ball. Now then, every male between the ages of 18 and 80 during that period sported a really bad, bushy handlebar moustache. It was ridiculous even to attempt to tell footballers apart. One sporting cove with red cheeks and a handlebar moustache tipping the ball over the bar looked pretty much like another. So, to avoid all doubt, the keeper was to be distinguished from the others not by a jersey but by a compulsory cap.

There it is: the origin of the cap-wearing goalie.

It's interesting how cheating – or the elimination of

cheating – has always been the main force in the game's evolution. This means that in all those pre-war photos, where you see goalies sporting a cloth cap, they do so not because the sun is in their eyes or to keep their ears warm, but because the goalie had to wear a cap to cut out the inevitable cheating.

Bewildered referee, *circa* 1871: 'Which of you is the true keeper?'

Entire team, as a man: 'I'm Spartacus!'

You get the idea.

So, after 1872, our cap-wearing goalkeeper is the single player on the park running around playing to the 'old rules' of handling the ball. What's more, he's not confined to the penalty area. (That came much later.) He could handle the ball – but not carry it – anywhere inside his own team's half of the pitch. Goalies could roam the field and launch an attack by punching the ball into the opponent's half. In a one-sided game, a keeper could spend most of the match on the offensive.

That all came to a sad end in 1912, when the FA put the goalkeeper in his box. Handling outside the penalty area was now ruled foul play. (I've written a letter to Fifa urging them to restore the roaming, punching goalkeeper. Two years on, I'm still awaiting a reply. Perhaps an email will come soon.)

Meanwhile, the shoulder charge against the keeper was still perfectly legitimate. Catching the ball in his penalty area, a goalie could be barged over the line by a burly striker. Consequently, keepers tended to punch the ball away instead of catch it. It wasn't until 1894 that the FA brought in a (yet another sodding) new law, which stated that a goalkeeper could only be charged when playing the ball, holding the ball or obstructing an opponent – but that meant you could still bundle the goalie over the line to score.

The answer to that: find a really big, fat bloke and stick him in goal.

Yes, put the fat bloke in goal, with his cloth cap, and watch the shoulder-charging forwards bounce off his blubbery belly. And if he's got a good punch on him, well, they'd better not have a glass jaw. The aggressive strikers didn't seem to think it was so funny to charge a goalkeeper now. Fat blokes rule, OK.

Every team needed their fat bloke. In fact, Sheffield United had the famous 22-stone goalkeeper William 'Fatty' Foulke playing for them between 1894 and 1904. Forget about tape, he actually dragged down a few crossbars in his time. He was also reputed to sit on opposition players who irritated him. A myth developed around Fatty Foulke, for some reason, that he fell on hard times and resorted to making a few pennies at a Blackpool Sands 'beat the goalie' attraction. There was no truth in it; like all of us, he just enjoyed a kickabout on the sand. He died of cirrhosis when he was only 42.

I displaced a fat bloke from the number 1 position when I was a student, working summer seasons at the Derbyshire Miners' Holiday Camp in Skegness. Butlins, just a stone's throw up the road, had Redcoats. We had Greencoats, and that's what I was. There's that colour again.

As a Greencoat, it was my job to organise the sandcastle competitions, assist with the magic show, run the glamorous grandmother pageant, stage the donkey derby and call the bingo numbers. It was a varied and challenging employment opportunity.

Now, Skegness is not the world's number-one tourist

attraction, but a clever marketing campaign during the Edwardian era had transformed, with the aid of a Jolly Fisherman logo, the bitter and unpredictable east coast wind into something healthful and desirable. Bracing, they called it. It's a testament to the British mentality of making the best of things – or to our cyclopean credulity – that hordes of working-class families, post-war and right up to the '70s, would pour into east coast holiday camps for their annual two weeks of grace and favour. I liked working there, mixing with the mining families who were on vacation and the rough-trade staff, and in two seasons I learned infinitely more about life than in all the several years I spent at university.

We had a staff football team comprising kitchen porters, security guards, bar staff and maybe one or two white collars from the halls of management. Despite my mining background, I arrived at the camp as the only college boy in town and was looked on as an oddity, so it was useful to be in the team, where suspicions were discarded and you were accepted by the lads. Being in the football team also neutralised the resentment felt by some staff towards the Greencoats, who were often dismissed as work-shy show ponies who did nothing but mince around, trying to look pretty.

Within a week of arriving, I had displaced the fat bloke who was masquerading as the goalkeeper at the time and settled into the team. (Sadly, the fat bloke hated me for the rest of the season. Such is life.) Each week, a team of holidaymakers (campers, they were called) was recruited to line up against us on a Wednesday afternoon. It was serious enough: we had a decent pitch – well, it was flat – and usually a fully qualified referee. These refs – coal miners who were perhaps beyond their playing days but who couldn't bear to leave the game behind – were of such dedication they would bring their officiating kit and shiny silver whistles on holiday with them and offer their services. The quality of the teams assembled from the campers was uneven, to say the least. They might include a couple of semi-pros, but invariably there'd be 11 men who turned out regularly for their pit-village teams and so the games were usually tight.

These were different times. It was a pre-Thatcher epoch. There were miners in the land; people manufactured things. British holiday camps were only just coming under serious threat from package holidays to the Costa Brava. The 'industrial fortnight' was a regionally designated period when the working-classes downed tools en masse and, rather than spend two weeks clipping their kids round the earhole, they whisked them off for a holiday by the sea.

The system operated so that miners from the same districts would be allocated a particular week at the camp. Thus, one week our football team got to line up against a stone-faced Barnsley XI; another week we'd get our shins kicked by Shirebrook's finest. The games generated a lot of interest amongst the players, but little beyond that, though there was good fun to be had in the pre- and post-match bragging and ragging over foaming pints of Federation Ale.

There was a smashing Geordie called Alan who befriended me at the holiday camp. He was well into his 30s, a tough ex-army guy with an Elvis haircut and tattoos on his forearms. (In the 1970s, only a certain stratum of the working classes sported tattoos and they tended to be the ship and anchor, or the skull and dagger, or images of the crucifixion – certainly not the Chinese ideograms and crack-whore designs in vogue today.) Alan was pretty cagey about his background, but when he found out I was at college, he was very keen for me to read a book called *The Ragged Trousered Philanthropists*, which he admitted he'd read in the nick but which he assured me had 'changed his life'. So keen was he for me to read the book and discuss it with him that he made a special trip into town to order me a copy from the local bookshop.

Alan worked behind the bar at the holiday camp and, with a glittering eye, he would often slip me a pint without taking any money, saying that Robert Tressell, the author of the book that had changed his life, would have approved. He said we were working for exploitative wages from pseudo-capitalists: 'Call it one in the eye for the runnin' dogs o' cap'talism, bonny lad!'

A Newcastle fan, he loved his football and was always up for a game against the holidaymakers. He was a solid left-footed defender, nails, always upbeat, a linchpin of the back four in front of me. We lost him when the season was only four weeks old.

One Wednesday afternoon, we were into the second half of a game against a robust team of Yorkshire miners (robust in Yorkshire dialect means: if I can't catch thee, I'll clog thee) and the score was pegged at 2–2, but with about 20 minutes of the game remaining, something odd happened.

The opposition attack broke through in an advanced position on my right-hand side. Alan was an experienced player and I could normally rely on him to keep shape and position in the back line, but on this occasion he went tearing across the penalty box in front of me with knitted brows and a strange concentrated expression on his face. He was going way too fast; something about him must have terrified the player in possession, who simply let the ball run out of play. I thought Alan was going to scythe the Yorkshireman for some real or imaginary offence he'd committed earlier in the game, but he didn't go anywhere near the bloke. He simply ran across him. There was a 4 ft wire-mesh fence around the field and he cleared it in a single jump, knees tucked high under his chin. It barely broke his stride. Beyond the fence lay a patch of scrubby, sandy wasteland. He kept on running through it, towards a caravan site adjacent to the holiday camp, where he finally disappeared among the first row of white caravans.

Behind him were three uniformed policemen, woefully unfit, who also jumped the fence in the simulated business of following him. I never saw Alan again, but I still have the copy of the book he gave me.

We could have done with his defensive prowess for Scottish week. Prior to the game, the players comprising the Scottish team were unusually interested in our tactical formation. They'd line up the pints for me and try to get a sense of our play.

'Are you up for it, Graham?'

'Ye look like ye can take a wee knock, ken, Graham?'

'Are you boys no' a wee bit soft, Graham?'

All good-natured, low-level early intimidation that you just throw right back. Then one of them asked me what line-up we were playing. Four at the back? Five across the middle? I tapped my nose and got a laugh, but the truth was we didn't have a plan. It was never that serious. It struck me that, behind the joshing and the free pints, these boys from Scotland were. And how.

The staff were billeted in grubby, shoddy, battery-hen accommodation well away from the main concourse of the camp and there we changed into our kit. I sensed something was wrong as I made my away towards the pitch across an utterly deserted holiday camp. It was quiet as the grave. Where the hell was everyone? Then I heard a murmuring, as I approached the pitch. Every camper – about 600 men, women, children and babes in arms – had turned out for the game, most of them equipped with Scottish flags. It was like Culloden. The flags were waved in the air like claymores. There was even a bloody piper in full regalia, pumping up his bagpipes. The Scottish team were rigged out in full international colours, with smart matching shorts and socks. They were already limbering up, passing the ball around in neat triangles, give-and-go, as it used to be called. Christ, I thought.

I was the first of the staff team to turn out. The crowd turned to face me as I approached. 'BOO!' Six hundred people catcalled my arrival. 'BOO!'

I actually thought they weren't going to allow me onto the pitch, but they parted and let me pass, screaming in my ear as I went trotting through to the grass. Kids were massed behind the nets and the noise showed no sign of abating, so I went jogging up to the centre circle, where the Scottish team were still limbering up.

'Ah, Graham! Just you against us today?' one of them said. 'Where's your cronies? Are they hiding from us?'

Good question. I looked around and saw them marching in a line towards the pitch, a motley crew in an assortment of red shirts and mismatched stockings. They had never before arrived as a team. They bloody well had been hiding, too, waiting for the last possible moment. The boos built to a crescendo as they trotted onto the pitch. To a chorus of catcalls and whistles, I jogged down to one end to receive a few warm-up shots.

When the ball went wide, the kids behind wouldn't let us have it back.

Luckily, a friendly face intervened and rescued the ball for us. It was Hughie, a man I'd met in the bar one night. He was an oral poet, otherwise illiterate. He could recite every known Robbie Burns poem perfectly and dozens of his own. This he did one night after the bar closed, when he invited me back to his chalet to meet his wife and, in hindsight, six or seven kids, all sleeping in a four-berth chalet.

Hughie threw me the ball. 'Keep a clean sheet, now, Graham!'

I'd never played before a crowd like this. Maybe that schoolboy final with the purple-faced groundsman was the tops, with its 50 or so spectators. During my college days, for most games there was no one but the captain's long-suffering girlfriend holding a bag of limp half-time oranges. As for the pub teams I played for, wives and girlfriends were never dumb enough to shiver on a touchline for the duration of a game. Here, it seemed like half of bonnie Scotland had turned up to breathe right down my neck and hurl abuse, coins and empty beer cans at us. I was about to find that one of the worst things about being a keeper is the proximity to spectators.

A warm-up shot went in. I had to dig in the back of the net to rescue it from all the kids there.

'You're f'kin useless, goalie,' trilled one reedy Scottish voice.

It was the kind that can shriek over the sound of 599 others. You sometimes get a warped piano like that; it can cut across an entire orchestra. I looked round the faces for its source. Somehow I expected to identify a little freckle-faced, flame-haired, gimlet-eyed brat in a tartan Tam o'

Shanter; all I saw was a sea of grinning faces. I recovered the ball and booted it out to one of my teammates.

I tipped another warm-up shot over the bar. There it was again.

'Yer f'kin useless, goalie. Should o' catched that!'

That bloody voice didn't let up for the whole 90 minutes. My first game in front of anything resembling a crowd and one little pipsqueak had me rattled. The kids were spilling onto the pitch by the posts; I had to try to command my area, so I tapped my boots hard against the post – the sort of thing you do to drive your foot snug into the toe of the leather – but it was an aggressive act, as if they weren't there. A couple of the parents called their kids back from the line and the nasty goalkeeper. I did a few warm-up jumps and used my studs to drag those now illegal post-markers on the six-yard line. I was telling the crowd behind me that they weren't there.

'That's no gonna help, cos yer f'kin useless, goalie!'

We got stomped. I think it was 7–1 before they took the foot off the gas. They were hopelessly superior. I made a couple of good saves, as you do when simply so many shots are coming at you, but save or goal, every time I was involved that pesky little Caledonian voice squeaked out behind me, telling me how useless I was. Plus they all did that moronic crescendo thing, designed to put the goalie off his dead-ball kick. Incredibly, the home crowds still do it at the highest levels of the game. It never works. But it did here, once. I shanked a kick and it was followed by gales of laughter.

But they played some lovely football, those Scottish players. Many of them were semi-professionals north of the border and in football you know instantly when you are playing out of your league. The worst thing for me as a goalkeeper was goal number three, and for some reason I've remembered it ever since.

At 2–0, I was having a respectable game, old wee squeaky behind me notwithstanding. But goal number three, a nicely weighted cross, was floated from the left and it was dropping in that most difficult place for a goalie – between the penalty spot and the six-yard line. I saw the Scottish centre-forward, the guy who'd been quizzing me about tactics the night before, loping in for a free unchallenged header.

You're a goalkeeper. You keep your eye on the ball. That is the unbreakable commandment. But this striker, seeing that he had plenty of time and was going to connect with the ball unchallenged, did something outrageous. As the ball was dropping, he took his eye off the ball and smiled a juicy, carnivorous smile right at me. For a moment, I was mesmerised. He smacked the ball hard with the middle of his forehead and I recovered just in time to flail at it, as it powered past me into the top corner. That's just taking the piss.

Of course, the Tartan Army went barmy. At 3–0, there's never usually a way back. Culloden had been commemorated, if not avenged. The English had been routed on their own bumpy, dry Skegness holiday-camp pitch.

After conceding four further goals from the rampant Scottish miners, I was glad to hear the final whistle. The cheering mob were already dispersing. I turned to pick my goalie bag out of the net, and there it was again.

'Goalie, I telled you, you were f'kin useless.'

I looked up. It was a tiny, frail old woman in a raincoat and transparent plastic headscarf, revealing half a dozen pink hair-curlers underneath it. She briefly poked her dentures out at me, before turning away with the rest of the satisfied crowd.

The smiling striker – the semi-pro who had played all game at a speed that put the rest of us in slow-mo, and who'd later added to the headed goal with a hat-trick – came up and put his arm around me. 'Aw, Graham, c'mon. I'll buy you a pint.'

My initial impressions of the England Writers' XI team were misplaced. No, that's not true: the team was crap, but of a standard by which I was lucky to be included at all. I knew I was only there because of the chronic shortage of writer-goalkeepers. (I felt like a rare breed: lesser-spotted or greater-crested, infrequent to these shores.)

The team might easily have been called English-speaking rather than English, since we were bolstered by three Americans and a Canadian. I say bolstered . . . Matt Weiland was an industrious midfielder, useful in any team. Canadian Craig Taylor was an athletic and aggressive winger. Two other Americans in the company were probably as useless as me, however, and did have me ruminating about the prospect of progress for soccer in the United States. Ben Markovitz, a lyrical novelist who has settled in England, is really a basketball player. Yet even at soccer no one can take the ball away from him. An implausibly tall, thin reed, with lightning-bolt veins throbbing at either temple on his balding pate, his dribbling prowess was thrilling. To see his skilful and mazy runs with the ball at his feet was a delight. The ball seemed to be superglued to his boots, as he slipped past one player and then another, then another. Heroic.

The trouble was that Ben would beat three players, turn 180 degrees and cheerfully head back towards his own goal, presumably looking for more small fry to beat, or as if he thought he was playing for some version of the Harlem Globetrotters who didn't need to score.

I wonder if it's too fanciful to make comparisons between the way people write and the way they play football. I'd love to possess just a fraction of Ben's writing flair, but not his football talents. His play seems to exemplify the more self-consciously 'literary' strand of fiction (and I'm not just talking about Ben's work here, by any means): glitzy adjectives and adverbs; long, mazy sentences; a pride in style rather than narrative intention. In other words, what I'd call overwriting. 'Literary fiction?' Brian Clough would never have said. 'Just get it in the onion bag.'

John Wray, another talented novelist from New York, showed terrific athletic running off the ball, but in puzzling diamond shapes that had even his own team bamboozled. It was dizzying just to watch him.

'Are these American soccer techniques?' I whispered to Matt, his fellow New Yorker.

Matt looked at me apologetically, with earnest and swimming eyes. 'Hell, no,' he answered back. 'I've never seen such stuff.'

In case this seems like an attack on American playing styles, let me counter by saying that Matt Weiland is a very different footballer. He's an editor rather than a writer, and this somehow manifests in his play. He's a classy midfielder, with good vision of the overall game; he knows when to put his foot on the ball to regulate the rhythm; his distribution is neat. In this sense, his play tidies up the huffing and puffing of some of the more expressive players. It's exactly what you need.

I think the rest of the world secretly wants the Americans to fail at soccer. If they ever do take to the sport full on, we know they will demolish everyone. The infrastructure for sport is simply way ahead in the US. The financial support and the coaching philosophy are a league in front. But while they resist, and continue to dub their arcane and incomprehensible minority sports a World Series, even though no one else in the entire world plays their games, we still have a chance.

Fear of taking the Americans seriously is what led to the absurd rumours about the host nation prior to the World Cup in 1994. The TV networks, it was whispered, were so powerful that they were demanding the game be staged in four quarter-periods instead of two forty-five-minute periods, so that advertising revenue could be increased.

'They can't do that!' I remember telling the little guy who had a season ticket for the seat next to me at Highfield Road. (After a lot of denial, I finally recognised the misery this was causing me and my family, and I went through a successful seven-step programme to help me lose my addiction to season tickets at Coventry.)

'And I'll tell you something else, and for nothing.' (Yes, a lot of people in Coventry are prepared to tell you things *for nothing*.) He wore a woolly hat pulled low over his ears. His nose was permanently made purple by exploded veins. He wagged his finger at me. 'In order to make sure there are plenty of goals, they're insisting on increasing the size of the goals.'

'Get out of here!'

'And I'll tell you something else for nothing. They're proposing the goalposts be fixed on wheels – castors – so that they can be extended if the game moves into extra time.'

'What? Where are you getting this from?'

He didn't answer. Instead he turned back to the game that was taking place in front of us and nodded his head, once, aggressively.

I shook my head at these absurd stories. But the trouble was, what with Americans being Americans, and what with capital being capital, and with advertising revenue already dictating the reshaping of the game in a deeply entrenched England, at the back of your mind you could catch yourself wondering . . . Hell, next thing we'd have lightweight balls that swerve in the air just to baffle the goalkeepers. Ha, ha! Just kidding!

The truth is that football in the States is on the slow march. Even back in 1994, the World Cup finals were watched by the highest number of live spectators *ever* in the history of the World Cup. What's more, it also had the highest attendance for a single sporting event in United States history. Read that last line again. And where do all the kids want to play? They want to play in goal.

Yes, they want to pull on the green smock. It's entirely congruent with American social history. American sports fans are attracted to the notion of heroic individualism. In football, there is no position analogous to that of the quarterback in American football, except for the position of the goalkeeper. Perhaps Americans identify with the performance of the individual above cooperative endeavour.

In his terrific book *The Damned Utd*, writer David Peace suggested that Brian Clough started to wear a green goalkeeper's sweater to wind up his predecessor at Leeds, Don Revie, who reputedly thought the colour was unlucky. But that's not true. It was from Clough's period of managing the great Peter Shilton and Cloughie thought his keeper was getting too big for his training boots. He stole his shirt and told Shilton, 'I'm the only number one around here, young man.'

If you look at the Premiership, there are almost as many American goalkeepers as there are English ones. And yet there are very few American outfielders plying their wares in the English Premiership. This means that the crème de la crème of American soccer players are goalkeepers.

And the American goalkeepers are superb. Consider these stats, published by the *Daily Telegraph* for the Premiership 2006–07 season. Marcus Hahnemann (USA) was the league leader in saves made, with 164, and third in save percentage, with 78.5 per cent, behind Tim Howard (USA) and Peter Cech. Brad Friedel (USA) was second in the league in saves made, with 153, and seventh in save percentage, with 73.9 per cent. Tim Howard (USA) was fourth on the list in saves made, with 134, and second on the list in save percentage, with 82.2 per cent, behind Peter Cech. Friedel's Blackburn finished tenth, Hahnemann's Reading finished eighth and Howard's Everton finished sixth. You might think that the lower down the table you finish, the more work the goalkeeper has had to do. If only Friedel were an Englishman, we would have solved our national goalkeeping crisis.

We're in the changing-room just before our first match in the Writers' World Cup in Florence. I'm lacing up my boots (whether to tie the lace conventionally or by looping the lace underneath the boot and knotting it at the side –

you'd think after all this time I might have settled these small questions, but no, apparently not) when John Wray, the American late addition to the team, settles himself next to me on the bench. Everyone else is limbering up, cupping their genitals, bouncing balls and mucking about with Deep Heat.

'Hey,' he whispers to me. 'You're the goal-tender, right?'

'Eh?'

'Goal-tender, that's you, right? That's why your shirt is a different colour.'

'Goalkeeper. Yes, goalkeeper.'

'Goalkeeper, right, right. I just wanted to check out with you a couple of points.'

John is certainly no slouch as a writer. He's been described as one of America's most promising young talents.

'Sure.'

'It's about the two boxes demarking your command area.'

'Penalty area.'

'Right, penalty areas. The penalty areas. What are they for?'

'What are they for? What are the penalty areas for?'

'Yeah, the two white boxes, huh?'

I gaze into his unblinking eyes. Then I realise he's taking the piss. I playfully cuff him round his ear.

He rubs his ear. Then I look into his eyes again. No, he isn't taking the piss. Americans in the large tend not to take the piss. It's not a commodity they deal in, generally. I've often tried to explain this curious English idiom to Americans, but it's not worth the time it takes.

'No, I know the big box is your command area, for handling the ball,' he says. 'What about the little box?'

'The six-yard box?'

The geometry of the football pitch – the white markings that grumpy groundsmen get so steamed up about – must look a bit mystifying to the uninitiated, the goalkeeper's penalty area in particular. But every mark is connected with the evolution of the game; even the halfway line was once a demarcation of nothing but the goalkeeper's powers.

Back at the end of the nineteenth century, the rules allowed the goalkeeper to use his hands expressly for the protection of his goal only. So, where does that 'protection' stop? Where does defensive play turn into offensive play? An FA memorandum made in 1887 for the *Guidance of Umpires and Referees* determined that the keeper couldn't possibly be *defending* his goal when he was in the opponent's half, therefore handling in the opponent's half was prohibited. And since it is difficult in a game without markers to determine exactly where a half begins and ends, the halfway line was introduced.

You didn't know that. Stop making out that you did.

The halfway line is (or rather was) the old-time goalkeeper's handling line. There was *no* penalty box at that time; however, there was a line 12 yards out from the goal-line (going right through where the penalty spot is now) all the way across the width of the pitch. There was no penalty spot, since penalties were taken from that line at a point nearest to the infringement.

The penalty kick (and the above penalty-kick line) was an idea suggested by the Irish Football Association in 1891. Before that in the public schools, there was an unwritten assumption that a gentleman would never deliberately break the rules. *Dash it all, Paddy, only a blackguard or a member of the lower orders would commit a deliberate foul!* Well, the Irish weren't having that load of old bollocks. There was to be added an optional (yes, optional markings!) broken 18-yard line behind which players had to stand when a penalty was kicked. So, when a goalkeeper's handling of the ball was ultimately pegged back, it was to this pre-existing 18-yard line.

The 'D' outside the penalty box is easy to explain. It didn't exist until 1937. You won't see a 'D' on photographs taken before then, so don't waste your time checking – they're not there. It is an arc drawn ten yards from the penalty spot, to stop players encroaching on the penalty kicker.

You getting all this, John? Because we're playing the Italians in five minutes and they're pretty good.

Now, the six-yard box, technically called the 'goal area', is a bit more mysterious in its origins. There was no six-yard box until 1902. Instead there were two intersecting circles drawn from the goalposts, looking like a pair of mammary glands. I wish they were still there – not because they look like mammary glands but because they would have given a goalkeeper a much better sense of his position, as opposed to the six-yard-box stud markings that had me falling foul of that purple-faced groundsman at the Butts stadium.

Apart from marking a line from where to take the goalkick, I've no earthly idea what the intersecting circles or the boxing of the six-yard line was or is all about. And no one can tell me. I've researched it. I've googled it. I've asked pipe-smoking old lags and I've consulted professional referees. No one, not even the FA, it seems, can answer this question properly. Why have an intersecting circle? No one knows. Why change it to a box? No one knows. So, while you're busy laughing at

Americans asking perfectly justifiable questions, just admit that you don't know either.

You take a goalkick from the six-yard line, but that doesn't explain why it's a box. The box really has nothing to do with the keeper. There is a rule that indirect free-kicks awarded to the attacking team within the six-yard box must be taken from the point on the six-yard line nearest to where the original incident occurred – surely, legislated after the existence of the box. So, there you are then. The six-yard box. *You* explain it to Americans, if you can. If you think you're hard enough.

There are some things in life – dark mysteries, like the immovability of a pernicious and destructive British class system, and the existence of the six-yard box – that are not meant to be explained. Just preserved.

Anyway, it was in the dressing-room, while I was still lacing my boots and contemplating the fact that at least one of our players was still coming to terms with the pitch markings, that Sam Taylor, eyes bright and thighs glowing with Deep Heat, bounced a ball in front of me and said, 'Albert Camus was a goalkeeper.'

'I know,' I replied.

'Is it for charity?'

It's my dad, shortly after the WD-40 dispute, still trying to get his head round the fact that this jaunt, this jamboree, this football junket, is all being sponsored. It's like free money: it makes no sense to him. Me neither, I must confess. I'm just playing.

'Is it like raising money for something or other?'

'No, Dad. It's all about spending money, I guess, not raising it.'

No, he still doesn't get it. Why would hard-earned money – the thing that drives you down a coal mine to sweat and grub in the earth in order to put food on the table for your kids, the thing that everyone fights over – be so carelessly strewn on the grass, as it were? My dad tugs aggressively at his ear, still trying to get a handle on what's going on.

'It's a different world, Dad, for these champagne socialists,' says my brother, Martin.

'What the hell has that got to do with anything?' I protest.

'That money, the cost of all these flights and all the rest of it,' he says firmly, 'could be put to sensible use.'

This passes for good sport in our house. My other brother, David, warms to it. 'Feeding starving kids in the Third World.'

'Digging wells. Clean drinking water.' Martin.

'Vaccinations.' David.

'Medicine. Schools.' Martin.

'Old-age pensioners' heating bills. Retired pit ponies. Save the aardvark.' David.

'I wouldn't go, myself,' says Martin. 'The politicians are crooks there. It's probably blood money. Wouldn't touch it.'

'Well, they're not sponsoring the tournament, so shut it.'

'Does your team want a first-aider?' says Martin, who learned his skills with a St John Ambulance brigade associated with the colliery. 'You probably do at your age. I'll come with my sponge bag.'

'He's a jammy bastard,' says David. 'He'll probably go to Italy and then write some crappy book about what a big laugh it is, all these crap over-the-hill writers playing football. One of them so-called funny books that isn't funny. And he'll probably get it published. For more money. From Rupert Murdoch.'

'So, let's get this straight,' David continues, turning his glare on me. 'Here am I installing energy efficient lightbulbs all over my house – which, incidentally, leave my home in darkness – and carefully recycling my scraps to reduce my carbon footprint, while you and 60 other fat-arsed writers freely jet around the globe, playing football matches that no one wants to watch. Have I got this straight?'

'That would be about it,' I confess.

My dad is still shaking his head. Martin is already slipping on his coat. 'Let's go to the pub,' he says. He jabs a finger in my direction. 'And it's *your* round.'

Imagine having to be the bloke who throws out the shirts for a Writers' XI football team. Phil Oltermann was and is that man. He tosses out the shirts, but there aren't that many tossers waiting to catch them; in fact, I think there were more kids mustered in my old primary-school classroom on a Friday afternoon than seemed to be available to play for *England*!

On the face of it, you'd think that the nation would be teeming with scribblers just itching to pull on the shirt. People think novelists are rare, but unfortunately we're ten a penny. Who do you think keeps those caverns-measureless-to-man warehouse-style coffee-scented bookstores plumped with stock when the average novel has a shelf life of a carton of milk? Who fills the libraries with thrillers and horrors and crimes and science fictions and chick-lit romances (oh, OK, romance writers aren't going to figure high in the team recruitment drive) by authors whose names you've never heard of? Who generously keeps the book remainder shops going with their donations? Then there are the legions of journalists, sporting and otherwise. Surely, you could assemble a dozen teams from football writers alone. No, it seems.

It's one thing to sneer from the touchline, quite another to get out there and put your head where it hurts. It's easy to have an opinion about whether the national team should play with five across the middle, quite another to make that mean something when you've got to make tired legs go where they will not.

Then there are the rules. In order to qualify to play in the Writers' World Cup tournament, you must have had at least one book published. Ruled out under this rubric supposedly are e-books, self-published works and books of poetry. (My heart leapt for joy when I saw the dismissal of the poets. New York journalist A.J. Liebling had it bang on when he said, 'Show me a poet, and I'll show you a shit.' I want Liebling on my team!) When I read on, my heart sank just a little to discover that poets would be allowed to play provided that they had published a book in another genre. What a get-out clause! And if you think I'm being harsh, you should listen to these poets read their dire and dismal offerings during appalling literary events forced down your throat after a vigorous afternoon game of football.

Most writers these days have *something* to say about football. Twenty years ago, following the fortunes of a football team was looked down upon as a brutish, plebeian pastime. Now, I find that every publishing meeting or launch party I go to has to be prefaced by ten minutes' male-bonding chatter about which team one follows. Give it a break, chaps! I follow Coventry City. They're crap, but at least they play in the town I come from. And do you really give a shit? I never say that, of course. I smile pleasantly at some Cambridge-educated ninny who claims to have followed Manchester United all his life. All through his days at Harrow.

In my writing career, I have only met two writers who had the backbone to say that anyone who enjoys watching a game of football is a moral idiot. These were Louis de Bernières and Howard Jacobson. I wanted to snarl back and cheer all at the same time. Naturally, I gave them an argument at the time because that's what they wanted, but they were right, of course. It is possible to be a stuck-up git about these things *and* be right. If they're wrong, how come I might be lying on a beautiful beach in Sardinia at 4.45 on a Saturday afternoon fretting about the result of a meaningless mid-table second-flight Coventry City fixture back home? If they're wrong, why do we pay absurdly inflated figures for Premier League seats, so that we can devote ourselves to drunk-drivers, wife-beaters, rapists, racist thugs and nightclub brawlers and fete them like Olympian gods?

Every scribbling cuckoo has to claim a club badge these days, and it's usually one of the big four, of course; but try to find a handful ready to step into a pair of boots and you're hard pressed. Phil Oltermann wrote to a few likely candidates with mixed results.

For me, the perfect example of one of these latter-day 'fans' was invited because he lives in Italy, where the tournament was taking place. He responded by accusing the writers involved of knowing nothing about football and doing it all for cheap publicity. (Note to posh cad: some of us have been kicking balls against the factory gates since we were small boys. Hard to fathom, huh?) Another professional comic initially signed up but allegedly dropped out when he discovered that the squad included a player who'd apparently given him a bad review a decade earlier. (Note to comic: you did the right thing – all the team are mean-mouthed sons o' bitches, and the reviewing in particular has got worse.)

The plain fact is that most writers are either introverts or take themselves too bloody seriously to play football. They're sensitive hot-house flowers. Obviously, they can talk a good game on their way to school, but when they get there they've always forgotten their kit.

There is a basic mismatch in the idea of the athlete and the notion of the aesthete. When I was at college, this gap was a pronounced one. On the one horny hand, you had your competitive athletes (what the Americans call jocks), who were mostly destined for careers as PE teachers, shouting at the kids who were pretending to have forgotten their kit; on the other hand, you had your effete academic types, swooning like little girls over literature, mostly destined for careers as English teachers, shouting at the kids who were pretending to have forgotten their books. I arrived at college in the former camp and crossed the floor, as they say in the Houses of Parliament, into the other, the swooning girls' one.

I regret not playing more football in my college days. I was good enough to play for the college side – and frequently did – but I missed a lot of great games because I couldn't stand the regularity of giving up my Saturday morning in bed. Look at it this way: you're 19 years old; you have your own pad for the first time in your life; there's drink, there are drugs, there are a million great books to read, and there is a ratio at your teacher-training college of six girls for every one bloke. Even Quasimodo could score with a ratio like that. And you want me to miss a Saturday morning lying in bed with my beautiful girlfriend to get muddy, wet and cold with a bunch of sweaty jocks? You're either insane or you are dithering and uncertain about your sexuality.

I remember being approached in the student union bar one evening by one of the sporting fraternity. He was vice-chairman of the Student Sports Council Recruitment Sub-Committee or something of that order. A likeable guy, he always stood his round, played football, rugby and hockey, did high jump, long jump and pole vault, along with shove-halfpenny and every other competitive game on the planet. Every muscle on his body rippled with rude health except for the one in his skull. I'd turned out for him on a casual basis one evening when the college football team was short of a goalkeeper and I had happened to play fairly well on that occasion, probably to his surprise.

He'd had too much to drink and he was having a go at me. 'People like you annoy me,' he was saying, wagging his finger in my face. 'You could make a contribution, but you can't be bothered. You just can't be bothered.'

'You're right,' I said. 'Nail me to the cross.'

He went away shaking his head sadly. But let's get this straight: I wasn't a dazzling prospect who could have gone on to play professional football. I was an OK but somewhat erratic goalie who didn't much enjoy turning out in the rain with a hangover, though I missed the cut and thrust of the game enough to allow myself to be 'on-call' – that is, if the regular and dedicated keeper couldn't make it, then I'd show up with bed-head. And sometimes worse.

I'd arranged one weekend for an old friend from back home to visit me and I'd promised him party time, regaling him with stories of cheap beer, good rock bands and the wildly favourable male–female ratio. Some time before he arrived, the college team captain had told me the regular keeper had cried off and asked if I could deputise. I'd already said I would, without thinking about my friend from home. The bloody idiot washed up on campus with a bag of LSD microdots.

I thought it would be OK. I calculated that an eight-hour trip, if I took the microdot early enough, wouldn't be too much trouble the next day. Come the morning of the game, the trip had subsided, but I was still experiencing strong visual hallucinations, in particular the common acid-phenomenon of the staggered image. You wave your hand in front of your face and it fans forward, so that you see not one arm but seven more identical arms following the trajectory of your 'real' arm. At breakfast, I drank a lot of orange juice, which is supposed to be an antidote. I had a cold shower and hoped the fresh air would clear my head.

It didn't.

In the pre-match warm-up, the balls were coming at me like tracer-fire. I could see the entire trajectory of a shot, like a comet with a long tail, punctuated by six or seven balls along its route. I said nothing to the team captain and prayed for a quiet time in the nets. As it happened, our team was dominant and I wasn't called on to do anything until at least ten minutes into the game, when one of the opposition midfielders lobbed a high, ineffective, speculative shot at me. I had lots of time to see it coming.

Of the many balls I could see tracking towards me, I decided to go for the middle one. Wrong. With my arms aloft and well positioned to take the virtual ball, I waved the real ball into the net from, oh, three yards away. They talk about keepers 'flapping' at the ball. I think I was making peace signs. I remember my team staring at me in disbelief.

I couldn't tell anyone what was happening. Social disapproval of illicit drugs from the sports jocks was much stronger than it would be today. (Heck, half the current England squad seem to be stoners. It's almost compulsory these days.) I decided to tough it out, and luckily I didn't have a lot to do.

At half-time, Bryn Martyn, a relentlessly cheerful ginger from Newport, came up to me as I feverishly sucked back my half-time orange and everyone else's I could grab.

'That's the first time I've seen you make a mistake,' he said. And then he added, 'In goal.'

I jogged back to the changing-room and ran my head under a freezing cold tap for ten minutes. I was just about OK for the second half. Just about.

It was a moment of *satori*, true insight. But the insight wasn't the gift of the acid; it didn't matter that this match was only a minor league game where the result was forgotten two days later by everyone involved: insight came from the burden of recognising that I was letting down ten other good blokes by being an utter prat.

It was the very last time I took the stupid drug.

As it happened, Phil Oltermann rounded up an intriguing bunch of blokes, all legitimately qualified to play by virtue of having published at least one book. Some, of course, had produced several books over a career, none more than Haydn Middleton, who, if you include all of his short books written for children, has over 70 titles under his belt – 70! At this rate, he's going to outstrip Enid Blyton. Haydn is just a couple of months younger than me, making me the oldest swinger in town. Well, in the team.

He fits perfectly my theory that footballers express their particular writing style on the pitch. He's the most productive player we have: a master of the flick-on, the short pass, the tidy play, an uncomplicated style. In the statistics for completed passes, he would be at the top. I'm going to have to do something about this theory; write about it or something. Anyway, it was a small relief to have another over-50 in the team.

Our other squad members were gathered up from various genres: a handful of novelists, including two horror writers; a children's writer; a sports writer; a travel writer; a couple of critics; a brace of biographers . . .

I will admit that the writing world is cursed by its share of *uphimselfness*, but, let's be honest, if you didn't have at least some *upyourselfness*, you couldn't be a writer in the first place. Anyone with the temerity to write, say, about goalkeeping when it is common knowledge what a crap goalkeeper he is, is a bit *uphimself*. But I don't just mean having an arrogant opinion; I mean something else.

I never thought about becoming a writer when I was a boy. The idea was absurd, and writers, if I ever thought about them, were among a number of comical, rouged and bewigged grotesques who helped populate the world, like buck-toothed church vicars or red-nosed lady magistrates, or town criers. They were part-pantomime. You couldn't possibly become one and you didn't particularly want to, either.

Heck, even by the time I was at college and it was clear that I'd artfully dodged a career busting coal down the pit, I thought that published writers were people who spent their working day attired in brocade dressing gowns, smoking cheroots. I imagined that your published writer would be someone who rose late, ate a leisurely breakfast of kedgeree while opening his fan mail with an engraved silver letter-knife, presented by a doting publisher, and then settled down to work at about midday. A paragraph of deathless prose might unfold over the course of the next two hours in a process of mystical unburdening, after which our heroic author would lie down to recover in a darkened room. All presumably before dressing for a formal dinner of venison and swan with the lady magistrate and the town crier.

Now hear this, as they say in old movies about Second World War US Navy ships: writing is graft. Most writers I know treat it pretty much like any other nine-to-five, though for some reason the profession fosters a culture and tradition where authors pretend they haven't had to work at it. (Hemingway wrote about this in *The Sun Also Rises*.) The pretending thing is true of writers all over the world, and you wouldn't have anything to do with our books if you knew the half of it.

I suppose there are a few who get away with doing very little. There are also a few who do indeed lie down in a darkened room after writing five or six sentences. My agent was even prepared to name names. But they would be the names of writers of a very different order from those who comprise the football team. The darkened-room variety is locked in an elective struggle to forge the soul of humanity, unlike the rest of us. They have access to an infinite number of adjectives and adverbs, and a personal destiny that, taken together, the rest of us find too weighty a sword to draw from the stone. They are called Literary Writers, and they are a species of writer completely in love with their own glandular honey and stickiness. Thank the B'jesus none of them are in our football team because we would have to punch them in the mouth every time they tried to speak.

There's something about the nerve-induced dressing-room banter, the teasing and the piss-taking, that's very good for anyone, but particularly for a writer who might be *uphimself.* I've already admitted that in my chosen profession there is a great deal of *uphimselfness* that comes with the territory; not so much in the oily workshops of genre writing or journalism, but it is rife in the elevated literary climes. The England Writers team has a number of highly accomplished and award-winning personalities drawn from across the profession – mainstream, genre, journalistic – and there is no *uphimselfness* at large. I think that playing football must unpick all egregious examples of *uphimselfness.* It's not possible to play football and recognise that you're pretty crap and then to go away and display *upyourselfness.* No *uphimself* person could survive the changing-room for a single minute.

So, we're assembled in the dressing-room before our very first game against the host nation for this Writers' World Cup tournament. The venue in Florence is impressive, with an operatic backdrop of blue sky and Tuscan hills. It's one of the training grounds of the Italian national team, no less. The Nigel Spackman fiasco apart, this is a team who have never played together, some of whom were only introduced to each other on the plane coming over. We have no idea of our ability as a unit, just a suspicion in common that we might be pretty bad. But at least everyone is smiling, up for it, ready for the fray.

Then someone goes serious and asks, 'What do we know about the Italian team?'

'Well . . .' says our captain, Tobias Jones. Toby is the winsome and clever young author of *The Dark Heart of Italy*, a travel book/exposé of some of the more disturbing features of this great culture. 'They're Italians.'

'Are you sure this is the time,' Nick Royle says, 'to be making such fine points.'

'What I'm saying is, they'll use every trick in the book.'

Every trick in the book. *Every trick in the book*! Well, we should know one or two things about books. But apart from deliberate diving and tugging your shirt and appealing for every silly throw-in, what are these tricks? I do know one. It's to do with penalties. Or rather it's to do with the saving of penalties.

My own image of myself as a penalty-saving goalkeeper was corrupted when I was 11. In an old mining town called Bedworth (reputed to have the highest number of pubs per capita in all the country; I want to call Bedworth 'gritty', but I already used that word for Keresley and, anyway, its character is more coal-slack than grit), I played in a summer tournament for another Keresley team, mostly assembled from the same lads who'd won the Coventry Shield that same year. We passed through the rounds and found ourselves in the final against a team from Collycroft. Both sides had run themselves to a standstill in reaching the final and a tired stalemate of 0–0 resulted. The thing would be decided, we were told by a grey-haired, sweat-streaked, tubby tournament pan-jandrum, on penalties.

Nothing 'official' was ever decided on penalties in those days. I think it was considered unfair and un-British. Only exhaustion had selected this method as a way in which everybody could go home and have their fish supper. So penalties it was, and it was to be instant death. There was none of this best-of-five routine. The first miss on one side would end it.

The heroic Keith Randle – really a young god, who later had trials for England schoolboys – stepped up for us, flicked his long, blond fringe out of his eyes, and without blinking slotted one in, low and hard to the right.

My turn to face their penalty kick.

A few weeks earlier, I'd stood behind the goal, watching the keeper for the Coventry Colliery team save a late penalty. After the restart, I expressed my astonishment to the keeper that he'd saved the shot. Goalkeepers just aren't expected to be able to do that. 'Oldest trick in the book, son,' he said to me. 'He looked in that corner, but put it in the other.'

I was fascinated. It was true; I'd stood behind the goal and seen the penalty kicker do exactly that. This vital and useful information got stored in my brain in An Important Place. But it wasn't enough; I wanted more. I pondered on this revelation for a few moments before asking the keeper, 'What other tricks are there?'

He turned round. 'Eh?'

'Other tricks. What other tricks can you tell me?'

He looked puzzled. 'Well . . .' He rubbed his goalkeeping gloves together and turned back to face his own game, which was ritually playing out the dying few minutes.

I tried again. 'You said it was the oldest trick in the book. What other tricks are in the book?'

The goalie looked at me again over his shoulder. He obviously wished he hadn't engaged in this conversation. 'What book?'

'The book you said. If that's the oldest trick, what are some of the others?'

The ball was way up the other end. He turned back to face me and wrinkled his nose. 'It's just a thing . . . figure of speech.'

I wasn't letting it go. 'There must be loads.'

'Well,' he said again. He rubbed vigorously behind his ear. 'Well . . .'

To the goalkeeper's relief, the final whistle went. He picked up his cap from behind the post, abandoning my inane questions, and jogged upfield to join his victorious mates.

It was maddening. I'd glimpsed a book with one giant insight. One. A huge book of infinite potential; a mythical, large leather-bound volume not unlike a Bible resting open on a golden lectern, but filled with empty pages.

Some weeks later, I'm facing that Collycroft penalty taker. Though I didn't know him at the time, we were soon to become teammates at Nicholas Chamberlaine comprehensive. His name was Phil Thompson, and he went on to play professionally in Australia. Like the rest of us, after playing half a dozen games that day he was knackered. He laid the ball down, stepped back, put his hands on his hips and looked meaningfully and for too long to my right. I knew he was going to go left and, even before he made contact with the ball, I was diving that way. My outstretched hand pushed the ball over the bar. I was carried aloft by my team for that save. It was a great moment for me. But that single save imbued me with a faulty image of myself as a good penalty stopper. I've never shaken it off, despite the fact that in the 40 years of football that followed I expressly failed to save a single other competitive penalty.

Look, it was my big day, and I'll spin it out as long as I want to, OK?

But what else, what else is inscribed on the time-scorched vellum pages of the leather-bound Book of Old Tricks that might be of help? David Seaman, no slouch when it came to saving penalties, offered this piece of advice when asked: 'Leave it as late as you can before diving.' Thanks, David. Who'd have thought of that? For helpfulness, it ranks with 'Try to save the shot' or 'Do your jolly best.' It certainly doesn't find its way into the Book of Old Tricks.

I've flicked through goalkeeping manuals and the advice you will find is 'Read the player's body language' or 'Dive with full conviction'. Gosh, I wouldn't have thought of those things either!

The point is, beyond schoolboy football, and unless the penalty taker is a real bozo, he's going to know that you know that if he looks left he might put it right, so surely he will try to double bluff you, which puts you back to square one. (Or whichever square the penalty spot was in when they invented the bizarre grid system for radio commentating, from where the phrase 'back to square one' derives.) The point is it's no use because I know that he knows that I know that he knows . . .

I'm currently writing up a Book of Naff Advice. There's a lot of it about.

We trot out of the changing-room into the Florentine sunshine. Clearly, it's another Italian trick to make us play in sweltering conditions. We're all much more accustomed to swilling around on wind-blasted, rain-slicked fields or scrambling in muddy goalmouths, where the earth has been churned the colour of stewed tea and is the consistency of dogshit. So, no rain and no mud. What's more, the pitch is AstroTurf, or whatever it's called nowadays. It's plastic. Admittedly, it's a sophisticated plastic, with fine woven simulated grass strands on a bed of rubber crumb, but it's still plastic. Fine for everyone else, but a goalkeeper's nightmare:

1. When you dive you get burns from a plastic pitch. Your skin is left looking and feeling like a peeled prawn. For a goalie, it's rubbish.

2. The ball skims off plastic, whereas real grass deadens the speed of the ball slightly. For a goalie, it's rubbish.

3. The ball bounces oddly on plastic and does things to you that should only happen when you're playing Holy Joe's, about which more later. It's rubbish, I tell you.

I would honestly slither and slide and slop around in the pig-manure and cabbage-patch farmyards we call football pitches on our English parks than play on these Subbuteo arenas that reduce everything to skill and dexterity. We don't want skill and dexterity, thanks very much. We want the desperate lunge. The hopeless scramble. The optimistic punt into the blue. The wild charge upfield. In short, we want it English-style, thud and blunder, block and tackle.

Well, forget that, because today, plastic pitch it is. No doubt the devious Italians will take advantage by *passing* the ball.

Before we kick-off, we go through a sublime ritual. We have to line up on the pitch while our names are solemnly read out across the stadium over the loudspeakers, each syllable carefully pronounced, with a few words about our books. Then we have to stand upright for the respective national anthems.

I'm not much of a monarchist, so I have trouble even mouthing the national anthem. (Can't we change it, please, and have 'Jerusalem'? Never mind the Women's Institute, they don't own it.) Now, it's always entertaining to see the close-ups of the real England squad doing the national anthem before a game. Some of them bawl it out, some of them look like five year olds moving their lips as they read a book. I look along the line and there's only *one* of our players singing. It's a disgrace. Someone should stop him.

The solitary vocalist is Nick Royle. He's bellowing it out at the top of his lungs, looking like he might burst into tears of pride at any moment. Embarrassment at this performance seems to have prompted the two players on either side of him to shuffle away a few inches.

'Nick, what the fuck are you doing?' I whisper to him.

He ignores me and sings even more lustily. It's painful. He knows all the words, too. Personally, I think it's because of his name. If he'd been born Nick Roundhead, or Nick Cromwell, he'd have been a passionate abolitionist. This is true.

When that's over and done with, we are photographed, and this is followed by the exchange of utterly useless, brightly coloured triangles of yellow string and man-made fibre that no one knows what to do with after the game. Pennants, that's the word. Thanks. Grazie. Here's one of ours. Have a brace of 'em.

The great thing about all this, the thing that makes *my* heart burst with pride in the telling, is that there is no one in the stadium to witness all this panoply. No one, apart from a couple of bored six-year-old bambinos who have wandered in to see what the hell is going on. Not counting the Italian team coach and the guy on the public address system, the gate attendance for this grand, international, full-ceremony, all-expenses-paid fixture? Two. Two six year olds. And they buggered off after ten minutes.

But we're still not done with the pre-match rituals. I don't know about the others, but by this time my nerves are jangling. Nervous? I'm practically swallowing my own tongue. I just want to kick a ball hard. Fucking get on with it! I want to shout. But now – get this – there is a ceremonial exchange of books. Bloody books! All of this stuff makes me want to take a huge bite out of the plastic pitch.

One of my novels has been translated into Italian, so someone fabulously lucky on the other side gets that. I am handed something in Italian, which, as far as I can make out, is a study of milk yield in Umbrian short-horned cattle.

Finally, we're allowed to go and kick a ball around in the goalmouth. What a relief! Goalies need to take a few shots and do some close ball work before the game in order to 'get their eye in'. There's no doubt that hand–eye–ball coordination warms up, that limbs stretch and loosen, but you need someone to take responsibility to do this with you, to stand on the six-yard line and feed you close shots, when all your forwards really want to do is smash the ball into the net. Smash, smash, smash. Funny that. Funny how they can all SMASH the ball into the net from close range when there is no opposition defender trying to stop them. Come the game, they probably won't get a single shot on target, but in those warm-up moments your forwards are supermen, lashing the ball past you from two yards out. Anyway, we would be doing all that if only we had a warm-up ball.

Now, here's one of those old tricks for the book. The Italians down the other end have seven warm-up balls, while we don't have *one*. They don't seem to want to part with any of their balls.

'Didn't you bring some?' one of their team shouts, when asked to release a ball.

Someone, maybe grey-haired Haydn Middleton, puts his hands to his mouth to make a megaphone. 'No, we didn't bring any nets, goalposts or plastic turf with us either.'

I like it when people are so clever they never have to resort to saying *you cunt*.

Well, we don't look like getting a ball, so we go on a warm-up run around the pitch instead. Grown men, all in a group: jog, leap, turn, jog. Bloody ridiculous. What difference is that going to make? It makes us look like a cohesive unit, I suppose, and we hope that it will fool the Italians for a few minutes.

The referee and his assistants, all in immaculate livery, stride out to the centre circle and a whistle is blown. While the two captains go up for the toss of the coin, the Italians are suddenly flushed by a wave of generosity. They roll a ball towards us so that we too can warm up. All 11 of us. I try to claim the ball for a bit of close handling work, but no, there isn't time. The team is instead called together for a group huddle.

They say huddle, but they mean cuddle.

What the hell is this cuddling thing? *Didn't do it down t'pit when I was a lad, shouldn't do it now.* Frankly, it's embarrassing. If you want to put your arms around each other, at least do it after the game, if you've earned a victory. I don't much go for cuddling hairy-arsed men who have so far done nothing to earn the bounty of my physical nearness. I don't know when it crept into the game; I think it was about the time people started drinking Budweiser beer in England. One minute you never saw it, then suddenly the rubbishy stuff was all over the place, along with the habit of hugging. And now you have to do it; you can't stand there in your goalie's shirt, refusing to go along with it. No, you have to lock your arms round the next man, stick your head down and your arse up, and listen to whatever gibberish the team captain has decided needs to be said.

Now, to be fair to Toby, the team captain, what was indeed then said wasn't his idea and I'm sure he would want that on record. Someone else had cooked it up. But to my astonishment, I heard the bass and rather fruity tones of Ben Markovitz, our American lyrical novelist, quoting the rousing lines of Clough.

Brian Clough? That heroic and arrogant former factory worker, who should have been England manager but who wasn't because the posh twerps at Lancaster Gate couldn't stand to employ someone who had more knowledge about football in his toenail than all of them had put together over their entire careers. That Clough?

No, not Brian Clough but Arthur Hugh Clough.

Err, who?

Who, indeed. You mean to say you know nothing of the Victorian socialist rhymester who penned the lines released like homing pigeons into the Tuscan air that day? Shame on you.

> Say not the struggle naught availeth,
> The labour and the wounds are vain,
> The enemy faints not, nor faileth,
> And as things have been they remain.

I'm sorry, I want to say. I'm sorry, I'm sorry, but what the fuck is this? My instinct, while this word-slinging is happening, is to look up and see what the hell is going on, but I can't because either side of me a teammate has me in a vicious and putatively team-bonding headlock. *Get off my neck!* I'm yoked to poetry.

For Christ's sake, Ben actually goes into a second verse! Quoth he:

> If hopes were dupes, fears may be liars;
> It may be, in yon smoke conceal'd,
> Your comrades chase e'en now the fliers,
> And, but for you, possess the field.

If there's going to be an award for theatricality and obscure literary reference in this tournament, we'll win it outright. As we finally come up for air from this disturbing oration, I notice that everyone looks a little red-faced. Whether this is from chronic embarrassment or lack of oxygen, I'm not certain. I glance at horror author Conrad Williams. He just shudders. Whitbread Award-winner Patrick Neate catches me with a look that exhorts me to say nothing.

So, there we are. I've had neither warm-up nor touch of the ball, but no worries, because I've been treated to two stanzas of Arthur Hugh Clough.

We're ready to kick off and I must, therefore, fortified by poetry, pull on my Gauntlets of Great Saving.

Goalkeeping gloves these days are miracles of technology. As a schoolboy, I *never* wore goalkeeping gloves. Even when it was lashing down, and the pitch was greased with rain and the ball buttered with yellow mud. Even during sub-zero temperatures and we were playing on a frozen pitch. Gloves? *Only girls 'ave gloves.*

There were, of course, dedicated goalkeeping gloves that you could buy, but they were prohibitively expensive. Ordinary woollen gloves were hopeless; they quickly became sodden and your hands felt like lumps of wood inside them. I'd also had a bad experience with domestic gloves, for which I've never forgiven my mother.

I was playing for the primary school one damp and frosty morning, and before leaving home she asked me if I had my gloves. I explained to her the uselessness of woollen gloves, whereupon she started to rummage through a drawer and produced a pair of leather, or rather *patent* leather ladies gloves. I was doubtful, but she assured me that they were warm and water-resistant and would be good for goalkeeping.

Why on earth did I think she might know even the first thing? She knew less about football than a convent nun. (Actually, I heard a story about a school staffed by nuns. One of them felt sorry for the lads, who yearned to play football at school, and since there was no male teacher to advise, this robust nun took down a book from the school library shelf and had the boys line up according to the textbook diagram of orthodox kick-off positions. But she wouldn't allow them to move an inch from those positions for the entire game.)

Anyway, there I was in goal, with my patent leather ladies gloves. The first innocuous shot that bounced towards me slipped from my grasp like a greased pig and ended up in the back of the net. I slung the gloves off in disgust. Just in case any of my teammates weren't quite clear about how I was excusing myself, I jumped up and down on them a few times for good measure. My real instinct was to abandon the game, run all the way home and karate chop my mother.

I managed to restrain myself from this course of action and played the rest of the game with a clean pair of hands. I got home after the game and as I walked through the door, the first thing my mum said to me was: 'How were your gloves?' It was a long time before I ever trusted a pair of gloves again.

Modern gloves are to goalkeeping what word processing is to a writer. To begin with, they swell the hand-surface area by 20 per cent. Fifa hates goalies so much, I'm surprised they haven't ruled that big gloves are illegal. If they get any bigger, they will. Gloves do have the unfortunate effect of making you look like a figure at the head of a Disney parade, but who cares? Secondly, the palm area is a foam formulation that has a lovely Spiderman-type sticky-web quality. Thirdly, the fingers of superior gloves are bone-backed. That is to say, the fingers have a plastic spine to help prevent your fingers being bent back by that rasping shot. Sprained fingers is a common occupational hazard when between the sticks. You could regularly get two or three sprains per game: not from falling on them, but by making a fingertip save. So, the modern goalie glove is bloody marvellous. If Fifa do try to do anything about them, we're all going on strike – official. So, there you are, Sepp Blatter: don't even think about it.

Adidas do a very nice, very expensive pair that lasted at least two games before the crap stitching came undone and I had to buy a new pair. I wrote to them about it. Their customer service department wrote a polite sod-off letter back to me. I won't repeat my response, which referred to some bad press Adidas has had in the past. No reply to date.

Though goalie trousers and goalie shorts and goalie shirts (with a bit of extra padding) are all easily available, good gloves – if you can find some, where the stitching doesn't fall apart after two games – really are worth the investment. The only other goalie 'equipment' is the jockey hat with a sun visor. You certainly must have one of these, but you must promise faithfully never ever to use it.

I'm forgetting the knee pads.

When I was a boy, the Russian goalkeeper Lev Yashin was touted everywhere as the World's Greatest Goalkeeper. He was trumpeted like the Undisputed World Heavyweight Goalkeeper, as if he'd gone toe-to-toe with all his contemporaries. And how could they know? Yashin spent his playing career behind the Iron Curtain, popping up in the West only for the World Cup tournaments. I suppose he must have impressed on those rare occasions when Western commentators got to see him; he certainly impressed me with his knee pads.

Yashin was a true hero of the Russian proletariat. He was only 12 years old when he packed his snap and went off to the metalwork factory in Moscow. In goal, he wore a fabulous all-black outfit that earned him nicknames such as the Black Spider, because he seemed to have so many extra arms, or the Black Panther, because of his grace and agility. But he was also a proper cloth-capped goalie, perhaps the last of that breed. He never appeared without his burnt-brick-coloured cloth cap. They don't make 'em like Lev Yashin any more.

He was the only goalkeeper ever to be made European Footballer of the Year, and that was back in 1963. (The fact that only one goalkeeper in half a century has ever won the award is absurd.) He was also awarded the Order of Lenin in his own country – not a casual decoration in Soviet Russia. It's not like the British honours system: you didn't get the Order of Lenin for going to the right school or for making a fortune from meat pies.

Yashin was master of the penalty save and was said to be breathtaking. He offered this great tip for young footballers, which I guess should really go in that Book of Old Tricks: 'Have a smoke to calm your nerves, then toss back a strong drink to tone your muscles.'

In fact, he was pretty good for quotes. He also said: 'The joy of seeing Yuri Gagarin flying in space is only superseded by the joy of a good penalty save.'

But never mind all that, never mind the footballing gongs and the Order of Lenin, there was some other much more significant detail I discovered about Lev Yashin when I was 12. He shared my birthday.

These things are not accidental. These details are significant. Well, they are to a 12 year old moronically open to seeing his destiny writ large not in the stars but in the stats of *Charles Buchan's Football Monthly*, once upon a time the only dedicated football journal available.

Same birthday. Exactly the same.

Well, if you can't see the momentous significance of this, I'm not even going to bother explaining it to you. I might also add that he was born the same year as my own 'you must be barmy' father. I'm not even going to go there, because a kind of paternal conspiracy unfolds. But there was this issue of the knee pads.

I wanted some. But you just couldn't find them, anywhere. Neither could you find goalkeepers' shirts with a number 1 on the back. Lev Yashin had one, but they just didn't seem to exist, as far as I could make out, outside of Soviet Russia. And my mother said she certainly wasn't going all the way to Moscow for one. Instead I had a rugby shirt handed down from a cousin and I got my mum to sew a white cotton number 1 on the back. She made a neat job of it, but in truth the number was a bit fiddling and small. Better than nothing.

I asked my mum to get me some knee pads for my birthday. She looked everywhere. In the '60s, you didn't get these aircraft-hangar-type sports stores stocked with cheap kit stitched by three year olds in India. Sports gear was expensive and you had to go to specialist sports boutiques. There was one in the Coventry shopping arcade in a tunnel of shops adjacent to a huge, noisy aviary. We went there.

'Knee pads?' the Brylcreemed assistant sniffed, looking down his nose at my moon face. 'We've got shin pads, but there's no call for knee pads.'

I felt stupid. 'Lev Yashin,' I countered.

'What's that?'

'Lev Yashin.'

He looked at my mother. 'What's 'e say?'

'I don't know,' said my mum. 'He says all sorts.'

'Does he?'

'Thank you, we'll have to look elsewhere.'

I asked my schoolteacher. He told me that Yashin would play on a lot of hard, bone-dry pitches and that knee pads weren't needed here. But I wasn't going to give up. I got hold of the smallest pair of shin pads I could find and strapped them to my knees with masking tape before a practice game. Rather than help me to play like Lev Yashin, they looked and felt bloody stupid. One of them fell off as I took a goalkick.

Lev, I might as well have tried to get close to the orbiting Yuri Gagarin.

But in Florence that day under the blazing sunshine, as the referee looked to both goalkeepers for the ready signal, it wasn't the skin on my knees that I was worried about. It was the tissue on the inside of my knees. I was just praying that they would give me the full 90 minutes.

Spring. A goalkeeper needs spring. Spring is the essential quality that gives vertical or horizontal impulsion when leaping for a shot. And the compression that makes spring possible comes from the knees. Even with the aerospace engineering formula of WD-40, I don't seem to have knees any more.

Dead-ball kicking makes things even worse. When taking a goalkick, your kicking knee obviously takes some hammer, but all the crunch force of your pivot lands on the other knee. Halfway through a game, my knees start to feel like they're made of broken glass, where the absence of cartilage means that bone is grinding on bone. The day after a game they lock and I limp.

My mate, Dave Tull, is a GP, and a good one. He comes from a family of London dockers and he calls a spade *a fing wot gardeners use*. I asked him what I could do.

'Give up football. Give up skiing.'

'Thanks a bunch.'

'Unless you've actually shredded your cartilage again, which you haven't, you could have a new knee made of plastic and metal implants. Believe me, you don't want that.'

'So much for modern medicine.'

'You're not 16 any more. Give it up, or carry on and take out shares in ibuprofen.'

Often you will hear a report of a goalkeeper being caught 'flat-footed' on failing to stop a shot. What this means is that the goalkeeper has allowed himself to rock back on his heels, whereas he needed to be poised on the balls of his feet, ready to spring when the shot comes in. Now, even if my stance is effective and I'm on the balls of my feet, my leap spring is weak.

I don't know when it went. It's a funny thing, but one day when you are in your 30s you might jump over a wall and on landing suddenly notice that the compression in your knees has vanished. (I don't know why a grown man should be jumping over a wall, but you never know when your wife is going to chase you down the garden path.) Something solidifies. My spring has sprung. I can't get the compression in my knees to make the leap that 20 years ago would have given me a couple of inches to add to my reach.

The other thing is my kick. I think I'm unconsciously pulling back to reduce the impact, but I can't get decent distance on my goalkicks. That's to say, I can drop the kicks just over the halfway line, but I used to get much better distance. It's all very well getting wise as you get older, but there is nothing like competitive sports to expose the body's ageing process. I can't be that wise, or I wouldn't keep denying that this is happening to me.

I go to visit my parents. My dad opens the door. He's recently been diagnosed with bladder cancer. He's fighting it. I kiss his cheek and he accepts it naturally – something that would never have happened with this burly coal miner 30 years ago. *Wha . . .? Get off of me, you great pansy!*

I remember well my dad striding onto the pitch in his prime. It was the only time I ever saw him play football. When I say the only time, I mean exactly that. He was never one for a kickabout in the back garden. Football just wasn't his sport. He was more interested in boxing, and would get down on his knees and spar with me and try to show me a few moves. Jab, jab, duck and weave. Or he would wrestle with me on the carpet and tie me up in knots in pin-downs with names like the Boston Crab. It was a time of hysterical giggles, but he had to be careful because he was immensely strong. For his job down the pit, he had to physically manhandle into place the huge steel rings that had replaced the old wooden pit props. His thighs were like tree trunks and the veins in his biceps were like steel hawsers.

One time when we were play-wrestling, a car went off the road opposite our house. We looked up and there was the vehicle, upside down in the bramble hedge lining the other side of the road, wheels spinning and engine smoking. He shouted at me to fetch his boots, as he dashed barefoot out of the house to go to help.

I found his boots and went after him, but he'd already

stepped into the brambles and was trying to get the driver's door open. We could see the driver inside, dazed but apparently OK – it was the son of one of my dad's workmates from the pit. The driver's door was buckled and wouldn't come open. So, my dad grabbed the metal panel at the hinge side and literally wrenched the door off its hinges. Then he gently lifted the driver out.

Well, that was it. My dad was a superhero.

There's a Mark Twain saying about how when you're a lad you think your father is strong and wise, then you hit your teens and you think he's a peasant, and then much later you realise that he is strong and wise after all. I'm going through that cycle myself with my own kids. I seem to have arrived at the peasant phase early, and with very little prospect of ever getting back to strong and wise. But I think I was about 12 that very first time I saw my dad step onto a football pitch.

It was a game organised for a miners' gala day in the sports grounds behind the Miners' Welfare Club. Just teams scratched together from the different districts to which they were assigned underground at Coventry Colliery. The thing that made me rub my eyes in disbelief was my dad's kit. It was begged and borrowed, and even though this was the 1960s it all had a pre-war look to it. His shirt was actually a rugby vest with a ridiculous large-winged collar. What's more, at a time when football shorts offered barely more buttock coverage than a G-string, the shorts he turned out in that day were some kind of faded army-surplus khakis reaching down to his knees, and which his meaty thighs were severely testing at the seams. Both knees were strapped up with orthopaedic support bandages. As for his football boots, I think I glanced at them and let out a little cry of anguish.

He must have dredged them up from the canal. They were museum pieces. Unlike the tapered and dynamic, sleek, black, low-ankle modern boots I'd had as a Christmas present that year, these clog-like appurtenances had a shiny, hard bulbous toecap and were stitched from stiff old tan leather that came halfway up the calf. They had six cork studs. And cleats.

Of course, it's easy to take the piss out of his kit when the fact is that any spare money had been put aside to buy *me* some decent sportswear; but you don't think that when you are 12 years old. You just die inside, and when anyone says, 'Is that your dad?', you lie and say, 'Christ, no, he's in the bar having a pint.'

I watched the game from behind my hands. It was a pretty agricultural affair all round. Dad got positioned somewhere at the back. He swung a stiff, splinted leg at the ball a couple of times, that's about it. He played with enthusiasm and I think his team might have even won; but to my 12-year-old eyes, he played with all the grace of a one-legged man in an arse-kicking competition. My superhero father had been exposed to deadly kryptonite, in the form of a leather-cased pig's bladder.

Actually, it never did matter to me that he couldn't play football to save his life. It didn't stop him from having opinions on the game anyway. But it does grieve me, all these years later, to see this courageous, strong man ailing, under attack from cancer. He was the rock, and as kids we were the waves splashing around him. Now I have to be like that for my own kids and it's hard to match up to his splendid example.

OK, writing for a living is not easy. But compared with busting coal every day of your life and doing overtime to pull in a few more quid so your kid can have decent football boots, it's a breeze and no mistake. Hell, I do get cross when I hear writers whining about the job and talking about 'suffering'. A Booker Prize winner on the radio was airily lamenting the fact that his dedication to writing had prevented him from being with his children as much as he would have liked. What in God's name does he think everyone else feels about work?

I never once heard my dad moan about how hard, or dirty or dangerous his job was. He never allowed his work to put him in a black mood. He was always, always buoyant, chipper. And I don't want this strong and courageous father of mine to go down to cancer.

He notices I'm limping slightly from the knee.

'You been playing football again?'

'Ar.'

'You must be bloody barmy.'

I never had a single moment of goalkeeper training as a boy. This is not surprising, since there was very little specialised training even for professional goalkeepers back in those days, never mind schoolboys. If I did stay behind after school for a rare 'training session', I was called on to do the same dribbling and passing routines that everyone else did. Give and go, give and go.

In fact, now I think about it, most of school PE, like art and music, was an utterly useless and incomprehensible waste of everybody's time. We didn't even get to play much football in PE. It was mostly conducted in the gymnasium. You'd spend 20 minutes getting out the exercise mats and 20 minutes putting them away again. The remaining five minutes of a lesson was spent showering after the exertions of getting out the mats.

Training, such as it was, lay in playing. You learned by experience. If you made technical errors without knowing it, these became part of your style. There was no one around to fix them. There are, of course, academies and after-school clubs now for boys, with the time and resources to look at training, but you have to pay for them. In those days, everything was underpinned by the generous nature of schoolteachers.

It seems incredible, but there were teachers who gave up a midweek evening and every Saturday morning of their own time to be there for a bunch of lads' football game. There would have been no fixtures, were it not for that support. Of course, Thatcherism came along in the 1980s, and with it came the selling-off of school playing fields all over the country; that and a mysterious downgrading of respect for the teaching profession (proceeding from the logic that if you were not ambitious for a huge salary – something of which teachers can never be accused – then you are worth less). Incredibly generous men and women, freely devoting their time and energy – did I ever once say thank you? I think I might have done. I hope I did.

At Keresley Newlands pit-village primary, Mr Ship used to pile us into the back of his minivan (wouldn't be allowed now, health and safety regulations) and drive us to a neighbouring school, ready to play. Four lads on either side in the back of the van, with knees tucked under our chins; one lad in the middle at the back; two in the front with Mr Ship. 'You all right in the back there?' he would shout before slamming the door shut. He was a lovely, gruff Yorkshireman. 'Too bad if you're not.' We were like illegal immigrants.

He'd collect the shirts up after the game so that he could launder them before the next one. 'Look at state o' that! Scrape mud off before you give it me.'

At Nicholas Chamberlaine comprehensive school, Mr Jacques and Mr Jones would either referee the game if it was a home fixture or run the line if we were playing away. This in sunshine or freezing, foul weather, without fail, utterly dependable.

The reason I'm banging on about this is because something else was going on besides the football. The commonality between the teacher and the lads was not school but football, the game. The pupil–teacher relationship was partially sloughed off for a while. It was important that we saw how grown-up men (other than our fathers) behaved outside the role given by the school. Here's a thought: I always worked better for teachers if I'd also played football for them. I know that there are many hundreds of teachers who still do give up their time in this way, but it's nothing like the organised, regular, full-on commitment that was offered back then. All that has gone the way of colliery bands, cricket teams, apprenticeships in industry, first-aid teams, church groups, young trade-union groups, and the hundred other ways in which a boy might see how mature men deport themselves.

I was 13 and we were playing Holy Joe's from Nuneaton. All right, St Joseph's. A home fixture on a Wednesday evening after school. Holy Joe's was a pretty tiny Catholic school, with a roll of maybe a fifth or a sixth of our juggernaut comprehensive, and the scores whenever we lined up against each other pretty much reflected that. I mean we would be expected to crush them 6–0 or

9–0, if we had a following wind. What's more, we were on equal points at the top of the table with – guess who – Keresley Newlands, the mining-fodder secondary-school team populated by all my old mates who had shared that primary-school triumph in the Coventry Shield. The fixture against lowly Holy Joe's, at the foot of the table, would give us a chance to go clear.

For all of the first half, I had very little to do; maybe one or two goalkicks to thump the ball upfield. For some reason, they hadn't been following the script because just before half-time the game was scoreless. Then one of their team lumped a useless long ball high in the air, dropping it on the edge of my penalty area. I casually advanced to collect it. It bounced clean over my head and into the net.

The whistle blew moments afterwards. My cheeks were still burning when I joined everyone for the half-time team talk. When I say burning, I mean they were actually stinging with shame. Mr Jones, the teacher responsible for the team, looked me hard in the eye. His own blue eyes were a holy terror to me. He put one large, leathery hand on the back of my neck and turned me around so that we were both facing the rest of the team. He didn't address me, he addressed them, and in a powerful accent that I now associate with Welsh Nonconformist preachers. There was the lilting quality of *hwyl* in his voice.

'*He's* the goalkeeper. *He* can't hide from *his* mistakes the way the rest of us can. *He's* a member of the team. When *he* makes a mistake, the team makes a mistake. *He's* got us out a hole before today. Now it's up to the team to put right *his* mistake.'

He released my neck and walked back to the touchline, where he stood with arms folded.

It would be a lovely end to this story if I could say that the team saved my blushes and that we recovered to spank Holy Joe's arse 5–1 or 6–1. But a stodgy game lumbered on without further score and ended 1–0 in their favour. Holy Joe's, bottom of the table, whipping boys, wooden-spoon artists, had come to our patch and undone us with a bounce that can still redden my cheeks 40 years later.

So, there's that moment before kick-off when the referee looks up and down the field for each goalkeeper's signal of readiness. The Florentine sky is blue. The sun is blazing. The whistle blows and, after 15 years, I'm back in action again. Creaky, but willing.

Within a few minutes, it is clear to me that we're in for a pretty torrid time. I feel a bit alarmed by how grimly competitive the Italians are. It's clear they urgently, desperately and passionately want to win. They dispute every throw-in, every corner, every free-kick. Off the field, they've been perfectly charming and sophisticated hosts. On the pitch, they have regressed. Football has uncovered the reptile brain. One of our forwards is so exasperated when they dispute a clear throw-in to us that I hear him shout, 'You're a writer, for God's sake. You're supposed to tell the truth.'

Competitiveness apart, they are stroking the ball around in fluid and graceful passing movements. Our boys are up for it, snapping at them, hustling, but we just can't get hold of the ball often enough. I can see a stamina problem ahead of us because our team is simply working too hard for little return. Twenty minutes later, my teammates are asking me to take my time over the goalkicks, to give them a breather.

Patrick Neate, with his shaved head and tough physique, is one of our strongest players. He drops back from midfield to signal for me to wait with the ball a moment. He's purple in the face.

Patrick fits the theory. He won the Whitbread Book Award, a much more hip, exciting and left-field award than the more famous Booker Prize. Patrick, though he's good enough, would never win the Booker because he's not depressed or depressing enough. To win the Booker, your tone has to be humourless and your ambition as a writer has to be to want everyone to utterly give up on life. Patrick's writing, like his football, is tough-minded, inventive, playful and clever.

'I'm trying to launch an attack,' I countered.

'No,' he said, 'that's real football. Don't do real football.'

OK. There is stuff you can do as a goalkeeper to waste the seconds. It's what, on stage, an actor would call 'business'. On the pitch, however, if you look like you're acting, the refereee will penalise you. But you can position the ball for a goalkick, step back, then walk up to the ball and reposition it all over again with a bit of backspin to assist flight. You can stamp on the earth to get rid of that divot – or blow away that speck of dust that has appeared on the plastic pitch. You can make a sun visor out of the flat of your hand, as you scope out the pitch, hunting for your target. You can bellow some meaningless instruction: 'Heads up!' or 'White ball!' or some such bollocks. It's all rubbish, all theatre, done so that you can slow the pace of the game. But Patrick is absolutely right: with only 20 minutes gone, our boys desperately need the pace to drop.

When your own players are tired, they start hiding. By which I mean they don't want the ball at that very minute, or they don't want to challenge for a ball at that precise moment. They turn their backs to your upfield kick, or they avoid eye contact, or both. There is nothing more dispiriting than taking a goalkick only to see it drop for a member of the opposing team unchallenged (I have no complaint to make: the boys have run their guts out), but when that starts happening, then the waves of attack against you begin to come at shorter intervals.

The Italians start shredding us with neat through-balls. Our terrific midfield guys are slowing, and what happens when the pressure drops on the opposition midfielders is that they have time and space to pick their passes. The ball gets slotted through the channels behind the defence for a nimble forward to run onto, leaving you one-on-one. It starts to happen over and over.

I can't see why the Italians are so superior to us. Surely, their pool of writers is no larger than ours. The imbalance is a bit embarrassing, though I should be able to guess at the explanation. They are cheating.

I mean rules is rules. It states clearly in the thing written on the back of an Italian beer mat that as a writer you must have published at least one book. Not one *article*, or an *unproduced* screenplay, or a wilting, bleeding *poem*. One book. So, how come Francesco Trento, a striker with sublime speed and an exquisite first touch, who just happens to be a former semi-pro, is in the team terrorising my defence, eh? Answer me that. E-book? Don't give me e-book. It's cheating.

Paolo Sollier is also on their team. Paolo Sollier! I mean, a former Serie A footballer. Holy cow! So, how come we haven't got a David Batty or a Matt Le Tissier? Hang on a minute, Sollier isn't a ringer because he's actually published a book, and a very good one, on corruption in Italian football. What I mean is . . . getting people who are . . . *good* . . . to play for you is cheating, isn't it? I mean you organise a football competition for writers. You don't expect anyone to be good. They're not supposed to be good. If anyone is good, it spoils it for everyone.

And before you let that stereotype about cheating Italians run away with you, let me tell you this. Sweden are also present at this tournament in Florence. Yes, and those fair-minded, social-democratic, perfect-society-formulating Swedes are also hell-bent on spoiling everything by turning up with good players. Niclas Kindvall, for Christ's sake, was one of the foremost players of his generation just ten years back. He played for the sodding national team. I mean the *real* national team, not a bunch of bloody overweight scribblers, alongside Henrik Larsson and Stefan Landberg. Jesus! And for Malmö FF and Hamburger SV. Let me tell you, a 30-yard screamer from that blond-haired side of beef is going to fry your fingertips and leave them cooking all night. Not satisfied with that, they have two more current semi-pro footballers, plus – get this – their two best players are semi-pros from frigging Finland.

These are the standards of play. And you can't shiver between the sticks, bleating, 'Help! Help!' You just have to play on. No wonder the Italians are strolling past us. And before you say anything, our inclusion of four players from the North American continent isn't cheating. It's . . . largesse.

So, the Italians are underpinned by former pros and semi-pros, and they are running us ragged. The speed and intuition of Francesco Trento on the left wing is slashing us open on these balls knocked up the channels; over and over. But somehow, somehow, I've jinxed him, and he knows it. He's come through one-on-one to me at least five times in the first half and he's failed to score. It's bothering him, and the longer it goes on, the more unlikely it is that he will. He knows this and I know this. Even if you're a crap goalkeeper, you can somehow jinx certain players. I don't know why.

He's left-footed and I know if I can show him just enough of the goal on my near post – but not so much that he can get a clear shot in – then he has to take the ball wide. He's tempted by it every time, and all his shots are either hitting me or the side netting, or are going wider still.

I'm saying this not to show how clever I am – we all know that – but to make the point again about the art of goalkeeping. Only half of the work involves actually stopping, smothering, deflecting or catching the ball. The rest of the time you can defend your goal successfully without even touching the ball; here the skill lies in making the forwards miss the target. Only goalkeepers understand this. And we are lonely in our knowledge. I would dearly love to hear a TV commentator say, 'Brilliant goalkeeping, and the goalkeeper never got anywhere near the ball.'

This is even more the case below the professional level, where a striker under pressure is more likely to miss what is after all a massive target than to find it. A goalkeeper's positioning can make even good strikers miss-aim their shot.

I can tempt Francesco onto the near post every time. I know it's getting to him, because with each miss he puts his hands on his hips and makes eye contact with me. And I like that, because each time he misses I know it will get harder for him.

Plus the frustration of the Italians is growing, and that's also to our advantage. They know they are slicing through us. They know that they are superior. But so far it's not manifesting in goals. One way this frustration does present itself is in the way they try to neutralise my presence at corners. So far I've done OK on crosses: collected a couple, punched a couple.

But then they earn another corner and a big guy comes trotting in to stand on me.

I must say that in most of my experience of goalkeeping, I've been fairly treated by even the most aggressive of opposition attack players. You are extremely vulnerable in two situations: one, when your feet are off the ground, and two, when your entire body is down on the ground. In the first situation, the slightest push can deflect your leap to take a ball. The worst I've experienced is a little nudge in the small of the back while I'm hanging in the air. It causes your neck to whiplash backwards. You instantly lose sight of the ball and usually you miss it altogether. On the ground, the attacking player follows through in a 50–50 – or less than 50–50 – situation.

Referees are good at protecting goalkeepers, but there is always the clever shit who knows the blindside, who knows exactly when your body is interposed between him and the ref, and who chooses that moment to commit the foul against you.

I played a couple of seasons for a team called Black Dog, named after the pub. Not Black Dog United or Black

Dog Nomads. Just Black Dog. It was in a lower league of the crudest Sunday morning park football. The team were a fine bunch of lads, who loved their football. But on-field they compensated for an absence of those silky skills with a policy of 'bruise and be bruised'. They were grass thugs: cloggers, hackers and choppers. They seemed to get through a packet of ciggies each in the changing-room alone. Some of them even produced six packs of lager from their sports bags and got fuelled up before the game. The dressing-room atmosphere and banter was evil. Often through the game one of my defence would go missing to relieve a full bladder. They'd stand behind the net – as if that gave them a bit of modest cover – pissing heartily.

'Not on the goalpost, you wanker!' I had to shout more than once. 'I don't want to dive nose-first on your piss!'

'Soz, Keeps.' He'd waddle away behind the goal a few feet, shorts round his knees, still pissing barely processed Stella Artois, steam rising in the frosty air.

All of the team had different coloured socks. It was that sort of league. But that also meant we came up against other teams of unskilled crunchers. One time I encountered a brawny striker with reeking armpits and one ear stud, who dedicated the first quarter of an hour of our match just trying to soften me up.

Within a minute of the kick-off, a long ball came through and I raced to the edge of my penalty area to beat the striker to the ball. It was an easy collect for me since he was a few yards off, but I went down to smother the ball with my chest – safety first. The striker came skidding in with his knees angled towards me, but also with his fist slightly raised. Shielded from the ref, he knuckled the underside of my chin with his closed fist. I wasn't much hurt by it, but I was astonished. This was a new one. (Take a note for the Book of Old Tricks: *No. 94 – The shielded uppercut to the prone goalie.*) I got up with the ball and laughed off his temerity. He just scowled back at me.

A few minutes later, a ball came through at chest height. I collected it easily enough at about the penalty spot. On he comes, and this time he dead-legged me halfway up my left thigh. I went down and the ref awarded me a free-kick.

Again, a few minutes later, the opposition win a corner. He positions himself on my toes. I step back, he steps back, hard on my toes again. I take another step back and so does he, so I nip back in front of him to reclaim my original position. All this nonsense happens while we're waiting for the corner kick to be taken. Other players around me are similarly jockeying and jostling for position, so there's too much going on for the ref to deal with. Now the ugly striker feels outwitted by what I've done, so he links my arm so that I won't be able to jump. I break free, turn around and, with two hands, I push him over the goal-line. 'Fuck off!'

The ref blows his whistle and comes pelting over. 'Now, now, lads!'

'Sort him out,' I tell the ref, in answer to which the striker starts bellowing at me.

'What you crying for, you bloody big baby! It's not a game for girls! You can't stop me standing in front of you!'

'Let's all just calm down,' says the ref.

I want to say, *It's all right for you, you're already calm.*

The corner finally comes over, I go up for it, and I get that nudge in the small of my back. My neck makes an audible snap, as it whiplashes back. I miss the ball entirely.

Fortunately, it's scrambled away. But I'm blazing. I glare at the ugly striker who puts his fingers up the sides of his nose at me before trotting away.

It's important not to retaliate in football. Retaliation is considered an offence more serious than the original provocation, which is quite right, because this is how things quickly get out of hand. When the ref sees it. The wise thing to do is to allow one of your team to run interference for you. The ref knows your blood is up and he's watching you carefully, so one of your boys gets the offender back for you, risking a caution himself, of course, but that's often the way that scores are settled.

I couldn't be arsed with that. I'd gone past the point. I'd turned out for a morning's leisurely football and I'd been punched, dead-legged, stamped on and whiplashed in the first quarter of an hour, and all I could think of was Bobby Gould.

I was just a lad watching Gould play at Coventry City one Saturday in what was the old second division, before Arsenal snapped him up in the transfer market. He was a decent but very physical striker. Years later, he came back to Coventry as manager and inflicted a lot of dreary long-ball football on Highfield Road. He was a better player than manager, and as a manager he has gone on record for a few ripe quotes. 'It's thrown a spanner in the fire,' was one of his memorable contributions. Or my favourite: 'We are really quite lucky this year because Christmas falls on Christmas Day.' Right.

OK, but as a player I liked him. He was a trier. An aggressive centre-forward in the old-fashioned mould, he was a worker not a shirker. A lot of it was huff and puff and bustle, but he injected energy into the game. He also had a habit of getting in goalkeepers' faces.

I can't recall who the opposition were that Saturday afternoon in the late '60s, but it was a dull agricultural tussle. Bobby Gould was hassling the away team goalkeeper every time he picked up the ball. Gould would stand in front of him, trying to block his drop kicks – something you're not allowed to do now. Anyway, Gould overstepped the mark with his shoulder charging and his constant hustling. At some point in the first half, the away team goalkeeper stood on the edge of his area, clutching the ball to his chest, while Gould got in close, like a boxer, actually trying to get his head between the ball and the goalie's arms, pushing, jostling, rubbing. Then the goalie let fly with a splendid right hook. Gould went down like he'd been shot.

Interestingly enough, he wasn't the only goalkeeper to fell Gould with a hook. Pretty much every keeper was enraged by Gould's antics, and Gary Sprake, the Leeds and Wales international, did exactly the same thing when Gould played for Arsenal. Dropped him with a hook.

Sprake somehow got away with a caution because the referee sympathised with him that day, but at Highfield Road the scene was different. I was standing right behind the goal where it happened, close enough to see the sweat on the players' brows and the fire in their eyes. Gould was out for the count and the goalkeeper that day was walking towards the tunnel, long before the referee appeared on the scene. I want to say the goalie was sent off, but he had already reached the touchline and had taken off his shirt by the time the ref caught up with him to send him off.

He knew what he was doing; he knew the consequences and was prepared to accept them. He walked. In a curious way, I feel as if he – and Gary Sprake – were acting on behalf of all goalkeepers everywhere.

Well, that day when I was playing for Black Dog against the guy with one ear stud and stinking armpits, I felt like walking, too. Football? Fuck it.

As it happened, I had to wait about 20 minutes before I got a chance, but my blood still hadn't cooled. We'd gone one ahead and they hustled another corner. We had a big, rangy Mancunian centre-half called Kev. Smashing bloke, and he was *nails*. When the ugly striker took up position right in front of me again, Kev winked at me and said, 'I'll stand on him.'

'No,' I muttered. 'Keep well away.'

Kev hitched an eyebrow at me, but took up his normal position at the back post instead. Just before the corner kick was made, I retreated to the far post. The ball came over and I went up to punch it hard. I missed the ball by about nine yards and accidentally smashed my fist down on the striker. I ended up hitting his ear, which wasn't my intention. I know I hit his ear because his ear stud gouged the back of my fist, and 20 years later I still have a small white scar on the back of my hand from where blood was drawn. The ugly striker went down hard, clutching his ear, while the loose ball fell to one of their players, who lashed it into the net.

I like to think that it is significant that the opposition team made their whooping celebrations without even a backward glance at their teammate, who was sprawled inside the six-yard box. I wanted to say, *What's up? It's not a game for girls* and all that, but I didn't get the chance because the ref immediately called me all the way over to the 18-yard line. 'Look,' he said, 'I'm not blind, I've seen what's gone on. He deserved it and you've lost a goal. But that's quits. Any more and you're off. Understood?'

'Perfectly.'

Just before the restart, big Kev looked at me with raised eyebrows, making a curious chewing motion, before, in a broad Mancunian drawl, he said, 'Are you 'appy in your work?' Well, I'd lost the plot, and we'd lost a goal. But at least the bloke didn't come near me again for the rest of the game.

I know it was wrong, but I did it for all goalkeepers everywhere. And I did it for the little people, those in the cheap seats.

As I say, most strikers don't bother you with this garbage, and if they're halfway decent players they really don't need to. It only happens in the lowest pub leagues and at the top professional level. So, with the Italians threatening the deluge, I'm a bit surprised when, as we prepare to defend a corner, one of the Italian writers starts mixing it.

I'm not mentioning his name because off the field he is charming, sophisticated, erudite and accomplished. Something about competitive football brings out the oddest traits in people. I want to say that your 'real' personality comes out, but that's inaccurate. It's a particular facet of a character under stress. Some people become braver than they are in general life; some get disheartened easily; some become bloody irritating moaners, constantly blaming their teammates instead of looking to their own performance; and some become plain ol' mean.

In this case, the member of the Italian team trots over and takes up position between me and my line as the corner kick is about to be taken. He grabs the sleeve of my shirt but also digs his fingernails into the underside of my bicep, gripping the flesh in what we used to call a cow bite (painful enough to leave a bruise). Now, I don't know about you, but I find that kind of thing quite unpleasant.

There are obvious things you can do as a goalie when people grab you to impede you from jumping for the ball – such as stamping on their foot or scraping your heel down the shin – but it all seems too extreme for the situation, when 20 minutes earlier we'd been swapping novels and reciting Clough. The other Clough. So, instead I quickly twist his ear very hard. I don't know why I do this. I only have a second or two in which to decide what to do and I think it seems like the sort of thing I can pass off as a joke. Well, not a joke, but a rough tease, in the same way you sometimes try to pass off cruel banter as a tease.

He gives a funny little squeal, high-pitched for such a big man. The corner flies in and is easily cleared by Nick Royle. Our defence moves out quickly, trying to counter-attack. I look round and my Italian friend is loitering on the goal-line, nursing his ear and looking at me with a hurt expression on his face. I don't want a conversation about what just happened, so I jog up to the edge of my area, screaming, 'Move out!' and 'Push up!' and all that crap at my teammates, which is faintly ridiculous since they've already done exactly those things a long time ago. Just when I'm wondering if he's going to make something of it, he trots back to his own half, holding his ear all the way.

The thing that disappointed me most about this was the idea that we couldn't have a game of football without us copying the cynical techniques of the professionals. Cheating. Dissembling. Faking. Diving. Shirt-tugging. Arm-grabbing. Elbow-locking. Ankle-tapping. Deliberately trying to get players sent off. All of it.

It's called the beautiful game, and so it is. And because of its beauty it is the world's number-one passion. But part of its beauty is the religious purity of its rules, and the rules are under constant onslaught from the forces of uglification. You can see a filthy, psychopathic tackle repeated over and over on television and the perpetrator's own manager will not even criticise him. Shirt-pulling, so hard to spot at the time but easy to identify in the replays, goes unpunished. Blatant diving, similarly identifiable, continues because the football authorities haven't got the spine to enforce retribution retrospectively, when they have plenty of video evidence to hand. I'm opposed to the idea of using video technology to make refereeing decisions, but I don't see why video evidence can't be brought to tribunals to eliminate cheating afterwards.

There has always been cheating in football – cheating is one element in the complex equation of human nature itself, and for that reason we'll never be entirely rid of it in football – but, of course, the problem is greatly exacerbated by the interests of big business. Millions of pounds are at stake for a team threatened with relegation. Success at the top end has a direct bearing on merchandise associated with a club. Premier League football in the UK isn't just about sport, it's a media in itself: a cross-over media of sport, merchandising, celebrity, fashion, comment, publishing (this book is part of that media), financial investment, political gesturing and internationalism. It happens to be a sport that now exists at the interface between media and banking. And bankers, as we all know, have been the biggest bunch of cheats around ever since the Bible identified usury as a sin.

My point is that just because the pros are caught up in big-business pressures and habitually resort to cheating as a consequence, we don't have to follow. We're just a bunch of chubby, middle-aged and out-of-condition writers having a good time. We're under no obligation to copy the antics of the football–media–business circus. We are footballers just as much as they are, even if we're crap. *They* don't own the game. *They* don't control the culture of football. *Their* uglification of the sport doesn't have to permeate our celebration of the beautiful game.

But we let them lead us.

My mate, Tanki, wants to give up taking the kids for soccer. He's had enough of the uglification, as it has filtered down to children: ugly parents, baying and bellowing from the touchline, taking all the fun out of the game. That's not encouragement.

Some of them also give him a hard time if he doesn't pick their boy for the team. 'You broke my lad's heart by leaving him out of the team,' one of the dads told him. 'Broke his heart.' I don't know what reply Tanki offered, but what he might have said is: 'Well, be grateful, because that gives you a chance to be a real dad, doesn't it? Gives you a chance to teach him something about life, to talk to him, to tell him that sometimes we don't get what we want, and that if we don't then we should work harder, practise more and give it our best effort in the hope that we get picked next time.

'As a dad, tell your son not to give up or to cry or to moan at the first little thing that goes wrong in his life. Tell him there's always the next game to aim for, and a hundred games beyond that. And, if he's willing, for you as a dad to spend a little more time with him, practising with him, making it fun whether he gets picked or not. It's called being a dad, and offering precious time and support to your boy, not being one of life's moaners whose first instinct is to look round to find someone else to blame. Like the team coach.'

Well, it's a bit of a long speech for real life. (Perhaps he should have something like that printed out on laminated card to hand out to crap dads.) In real life people don't make long speeches, they just walk away with a flat expression on their faces, wondering why they're giving up their free time for an idiot who thinks being a man is about controlling the world.

It's like telling your kids about winning and losing. Sometimes it's just not your turn to win, and it really doesn't matter if you did your very best and you had fun doing it. But, of course, it does matter to the Masters of the Universe, who have lately come to feast on the liver of football. They've made a bloodbath out of all notions of fair play, and the money awash in the game has corrupted many.

It was my friend on the Italian team, Paolo Verri, who advanced the idea that the writers' league in some small way had an important role. He suggested that as writers we should start with ourselves and avoid buying into the cynicism that has consumed football; that at least in our own games we could keep a check on the ugly dimensions of the human psyche that are so exposed through football. Play a scrupulously fair game. Be generous to our opponents. Control our petulant tempers.

We sip our beer and passionately agree with each other. Though it's much easier to agree on these things when off the pitch.

Gary Sprake has suffered more than any other goalkeeper from the curse of Holy Joe. He's remembered as a clown, when in fact he was a brilliant and accomplished goalkeeper. He is also one of the very few players who has had the guts to speak out about former Leeds and England manager Don Revie's alleged attempt to bribe the opposition into throwing games against Leeds United. As a consequence, Sprake was frozen out of the Leeds family. The allegation about bribery was initially made back in 1972 by the *Daily Mirror*. Don Revie successfully took legal action against the newspaper. Since that time Frank McLintock, Bob Stokoe and Gary Sprake, amongst numerous others, have all confirmed that the original allegations were true.

This sort of corruption we tend to think of as more Italian in character; the bitter truth is that we British are just better at hiding our corruption. Better brush, thicker carpet. The Mafia code of *omertà* is a babbling marketplace compared with the secrecy inside our professional game.

Sprake is remembered for a spectacular goalkeeping howler by throwing the ball into his own net. It was at Anfield, of all places, on a cold, wet pitch. Sprake gathered the greasy ball and, under no pressure, attempted to launch an attack with a quick overarm throw. Somehow, he either changed his mind or failed to release the ball and, while following through on the trajectory of his throw, ended up tossing it into his own net. An utterly incredible own goal.

Rumour has it that the Kop wittily broke into a chorus of 'Careless Hands', a true stinker of a song by the smooth old crooner Des O'Connor. Rumour is wrong again. It was, in fact, a clever DJ who played the song at half-time. Sprake – who, as I say, was in reality a quality custodian and no more erratic than most keepers – was never really able to live it down.

But he's not the only one. Holy Joe flaps his wings and crouches on the crossbar, like a demon or a big fat crow, and the best thing you can say about him is that he dispenses the howlers equally amongst the great, the rubbish and the mediocre alike.

England goalkeeper Paul Robinson suffered recently when an innocuous ball passed back to him by Gary 'Smiler' Neville hit a tiny divot and skipped over his foot. Unbelievable, and inevitable. Every game that every goalkeeper plays is potentially a disaster. Holy Joe is always behind you, digging your grave, measuring you up for your coffin.

I'm not going into any more of my gaffes, howlers, fumbles and blunders. There are too many of them and they're too painful to recall. But if Gary Sprake should be remembered for anything, it's for the clean pair of hands he showed over a scandal that many people in football – disgracefully – have refused to face up to even 30 years later.

At least in Italy they sometimes get busted for it. In England, never.

I seem to be bellowing a great deal at my defence. Shouting. Not criticising, but encouraging and marshalling a response to an attack. You're in a unique position in the goalmouth and are better placed to see the attack patterns develop in front of you. You can see danger, you spot the hole, you can be aware of the quick-run right shoulder and the lurking-threat left shoulder that your full-backs can't always see. You can also exhort your players to challenge, jockey, press and keep shape.

The worst scenario is when an attacking player has time on the ball to pick his spot and make an unhurried shot or defence-splitting pass from in or near the penalty box. Quite often your defenders, either through exhaustion, positional doubt or simple hesitation, will stand off an oncoming attacker, hoping at best maybe to block a shot. This is more than unhelpful; at worst, it usually just un-sights you as the goalkeeper, with the result that you don't see the flight of the shot until it's too late. You need to bark at your defenders, throwing them into aggressive action. Most defenders welcome this: the aggressive command from behind actually helps galvanise them into action. I often tell my defenders that I don't mind whether they actually get the ball, so long as they stay on their feet, keep their bodies goal-side and get in the face of the oncoming attacker. Then they are doing their job. As a goalie, I want to see strikers hurried into making their shot or hassled into an error. Thus, part of the goalkeeper's job is to have a BIG MOUTH to motivate his defenders.

I'm glad to have horror writers Nick Royle and Conrad Williams in the team. They are just so dependable. Actually, to call them horror writers might suggest that in football they are bloodthirsty, inelegant cloggers. Quite the contrary. Nick plays tidy, aggressive football, with fantastic sticking power. You know if you've been in a tackle with him: like his stories, he sticks with you forever. Conrad is tough and resilient, and is capable of inspirational moments. You can see I'm really warming to this 'football equals writing' thing. I must patent it as an idea.

Where was I? Ah, yes, mouthing off.

As I say, most defenders welcome the 'big mouth' support from behind them. But not all. One of my defenders is Jed Novick, the guy on the plane who looked like he was in a travelling rock band. I am rooming with him in Florence and learn that as well as being a great guy he's an accomplished biographer. He's written lots of stuff on comedy and comedians, including Benny Hill, he tells me.

Now, with Jed in front of me at right-back, I wish I hadn't heard that snippet of information. I already love this guy like a brother, but, let it be said, he's carrying more weight than he should be. His long hair, tied back in a ponytail, is now plastered to his neck with sweat. And even if he was in tip-top condition, he's up against their zippy semi-pro left-winger. Something in this formula keeps tripping that bloody silly tune in my head – the theme to *The Benny Hill Show*, the one that used to come on at the end of the show while Benny Hill was chasing half-naked women round the park, or they were chasing him. I'm supposed to be playing football and that fucking tune won't go away. I just want Jed to get in the guy's face, to hassle him, to jockey him, to dog him everywhere, but Jed is inclined to dive in and get skinned.

'Stay goal-side, Jed!' I'm shouting. 'Stay on your feet! Press him!'

It's the sort of mouthing off I do to all my defenders. It's not criticism, nor is it even tactical. It's just designed to dispel hesitation, to get the defender to find that extra ounce of energy to stay upright for the danger.

Jed, hooked on writers' dialogue or something, seems to think this is an invitation or opportunity to have a sophisticated discussion with me about the current proceedings. An authorial intrusion, as it were. You have to understand that at any split-second the Italian danger man might shoot, shimmy through or lay off a pass for another striker to shoot.

'I'm here,' Jed shouts back. 'I'm in position, I'm on him. I'm, as you see, fully goal-side.'

What? I think. 'Just stay on your feet!'

'I'm here, fully on my feet, upright, *Homo erectus*. I'm not going anywhere.'

The Italian danger man cuts through all this chat by taking a snap shot at my near post. It whistles just wide. Jed smiles at me.

Informative commentary, Jed. Full media-style self-coverage, and accurate reportage, too. It's just not exactly what I'm used to. I want to say a bad word at him. Not one Benny Hill could have used before the watershed.

When the Italians do break through – inevitably – it's not Francesco who scores (he's still jinxed out), but it's the same ball threaded neatly between our tiring back line, though played on the other side, to my left. I come out, and the oncoming forward steps round me and tucks the ball away to my right. One–nil.

They go delirious. They wheel away in formation like an aerobatic display team: the Blue Arrows. They kiss their shirt crests; they slobber over each other; they salute the azure heavens; on their knees, they praise their grandmothers and cry out the names of their ancestors.

Christ, it's only a game of football! We're only a squad of middle-aged scribblers, you great hairy wazzocks! You big bawling babies. Bloody wops. Where were you in the war? Etc., etc. I pick the ball out of the net. (I always like to pick it out quickly and get rid of it, for volcanic psychological reasons.) I boot it up the pitch and twang my hamstring. There's nothing like an anger twang in the ham to really make you sigh.

It's no one's error. It's just pressure. We're actually doing quite well to keep it down to one. So, at half-time we go in just 1–0 down, but with big trouble ahead. The team, me included, are purple-faced, gasping for water like that goldfish Peter Hobbs from across the road dropped on the pavement on the way back from the funfair. You know, when we were about seven. Or eight. Anyway, like that. Grown men, famous writers, gulp, gulp, gulp with the water, all agreeing we should have brought a few more substitutes. Another 11. Gulp, gulp, gulp.

Toby, team captain, reaches for some water on the bench beside me and whispers, so that the others might not overhear, 'What's wrong with the set-up, Graham? How can we put this right?'

I don't know why he thought I might have some tactical ideas. All I knew was that it wasn't about tactics. Our lads had run their guts out, and you didn't need to be a tactician to see what was going to happen after half-time. Add to the general exhaustion the fact that as a team we'd never played together. Teams get better by supporting each other's strengths and covering for each other's weaknesses. You get to know what someone can do, can't do, might do and bloody well quite probably will do. I wanted to tell Toby, what we should do is get a fresh set of players who aren't coughing up nicotine that was deposited on their lungs two decades earlier back in their college days. But it's all very well remarking on other people's fitness when, as the goalkeeper, you're not called on to cover a fraction of the turf that outfield players have to, and at pace.

The only thing I could suggest was to make maximum use of the rolling substitute allowance, to give dead legs a breather. In any event, Toby probably had a way better idea of what to do than I had. His writing is shipshape, keen-eyed, intellectual but snappy, and with good all-round vision; his playing is all that, too. His energy on the pitch was vital to us, but even he was running out of ideas.

I glance over at the Italians. While we are slumped and melting into the plastic pitch, they are all on their feet. The old Serie A fox, Paolo Sollier, is gesticulating vigorously and reformulating his squad. Even though I don't speak a word of Italian, I can read his lips. *Stretch-a them wide*, he is saying, *pull them a-ragged. Kick-a their sorry fat English butts. They're fucked.*

As a goalkeeper, I've never developed a strong sense of tactical play. I've only been concerned about keeping the shape of a back wall (which is usually four players) and what happens immediately in front of the back wall. A mouthy goalkeeper should help his defenders to stop them being pulled out too wide or from hanging around too deep. The decision on whether to keep a high line is, of course, determined by what is happening in the midfield. If the defensive line is deep, there has to be more pressure on the opposition from your midfielders. Beyond that, all the mid-to-front-line tactics of the game are only what I've heard in the talk of TV pundits. And, as we all know, TV pundits mostly talk contradictory bollocks.

For all the talk of 4-3-3, 4-2-4 and the rest of it, there is only one absolute. When your team is defending – when the opposition has the ball – there is only one formation, and that is 4-5-1. There is nothing else. You do not want to see your lazy bastard forwards with their hands on their hips looking back, recreationally, as it were, to see how things develop. No, when your team is defending, only one forward stays up front with his back to the opposition goal: to receive, hold and feed. That's when your 4-3-3 or whatever comes into play, in an attacking situation after you've recovered possession. This is not the same as playing defensively, such as a team like Andorra might against England, staying behind the ball even in an attacking situation. This is basic to football.

But it's not happening because we're knackered.

Another thing is as clear to me as it was to my grandmother: if you don't get a shot on goal, you won't score. And we'd just gone an entire half against the Italians without getting in a single strike.

Gelati.

But were we downhearted? No! The spirit of the team was frothy; we were knackered, overrun, but just glad to be there and working incredibly hard for each other. Was Carlton Palmer the manager who said, 'I'm not asking for more than 100 per cent'? Anyway, the work rate was there and the lads were enjoying themselves. Well, their hearts were having a good time, even if their feet wanted to go home and put on hand-embroidered silk writing slippers.

It is possible to have a good time playing football even when you're getting thrashed. But it's not easy, and for some it's impossible. The problem is that football is all about hostility: tamed, codified and contained, but it's still hostility. You can't really play properly if you don't have any. But if you're unable to regulate the hostility in yourself, then you shouldn't be playing, you should be lying on a couch somewhere, blubbing about your childhood to an analyst with a fob watch and a goatee beard.

During the '80s, I was still playing pub football intermittently, but one regular fixture was turning out for the Clarendon Park Strollers on Victoria Park in Leicester. This was a lovely, relaxed, coats-down game in the park, genuinely open to and populated by all-comers on Sunday mornings. It started with a group of mates who fancied an unserious kickabout before the pubs opened, and then it grew.

Any casual game on a park, if it looks fun, will attract attention from bystanders or passers-by. If anyone looked wistful enough, we invited them to join in. No one was discouraged, young or old, male or female. You could have been a snake-handling Bible fundamentalist and no one would have minded, so long as you left the snake and the Bible at home. Well, we didn't have a snake handler, but we did have disabled players, and a florid array of nationalities and religions. We had Sikhs whose turbans flew off when they headed the ball, and once a Buddhist monk in saffron robes and sandals who was visiting the local university from Thailand. We had a barefoot schizophrenic with pink-painted toenails who – and I wish I was making this up – berated himself in the third person for the entire game. Sometimes we could only muster five-a-side and some weeks we had eighteen or twenty per side. We just moved the coats back and extended the pitch. It became an institution. It survived for several years.

One guy, a regular Stroller during those couple of years, shook our hands after a game and said he was sad to announce that he was moving out of the area through work. We all said our goodbyes and wished him well.

Three years later, he reappeared for the Sunday morning kickabout.

'Hello, Jim! Haven't seen you in a while. Where you been?' someone shouted.

'Kuala Lumpur, Bahrain, Karachi, Singapore and Hong Kong. Then Taiwan for six months.'

'Right, well, you're kicking thataway.'

What pulled everyone in was not just the open acceptance of strangers but also a great ethos. Play abided by certain unwritten rules. For example, if a ball even so much as touched a coat-goalpost, it didn't count, so we avoided lots of pointless debate about whether the ball might have gone in off a real post. Secondly, if the defending team so much as disputed a goal, then it didn't count either. Everyone played with gritty determination, but what the hell did the score matter? People just lost count, and every week the game was resolved by the old schoolboy solution of 'next goal is the winner'.

Some people clicked into this stuff immediately, some didn't. Quite often we'd shove some little kid in goal. Maybe it would be a ten year old with cerebral palsy. (As the emotionally retarded thirty-something I didn't want to keep goal at this level, though we all used to take it in turns.) Then some bruising dimwit newcomer with low self-esteem, not picking up on the Strollers' ethos, would find himself in a scoring position and would blast the ball at ninety miles an hour past the shivering little boy in goal and proceed to race back downfield, punching the air, saluting the imaginary crowd and shrieking at the wind.

We had a Thalidomide player, a good friend called Graham Kelly. He had no right arm and a diminutive limb up near his left shoulder. He was a very fine footballer – far better than most of us – and his balance was exceptional. He was very difficult to shake off the ball. But such was the mood of political correctness at the time that it was felt appropriate that he should take his turn in goal. Like it would be some kind of discrimination against his disability if he was allowed not to take his turn as goalkeeper. Certainly he didn't object. This is what a slavish adherence to abstract ideological principles can lead to: an armless goalkeeper.

We'd been playing like this for a couple of years when one of the park ground-staff (another costive and curmudgeonly git; where do they find these people?) approached us. We used the marked pitches to play on, but without proper goalposts and nets. Would we not do so? he asked.

'Why not?'

'You're digging up the pitch for the real footballers.'

'Real footballers? 'Pon my very soul and how very dare you sir! These gentlemen and ladies you see finely arrayed before your gaze are indeed real footballers. Sire, we are all real footballers under God's grace, even if we do have fifteen-a-side today.'

He stared at us. 'You know perfectly well what I mean. The real players.'

'Real? Are we not real?' Our schizophrenic friend wasn't there that day, but the Buddhist monk happened to be. Maybe that's what had attracted the groundsman. (I thought the Buddhist monk could have given him an interesting debate about what was real and what was illusion in the great karmic wheel of life, but we didn't go there. Shame.)

'You know what I'm saying. I want you to keep off the pitches.'

This presented a problem. Almost the entire park was

marked out as football pitches. 'So where do you reckon we would play instead?'

He scratched his head and pointed to a clump of bushes. 'Somewhere over there,' he suggested.

'Bugger off,' someone said. 'Look, we pay our rates for the maintenance of these pitches.'

'Is it because he's a Sikh?' someone said, pointing to Jazwinder in his turban. 'Or because she's a girl? Or because he's black? Or is it because he's disabled?'

'Discrimination,' someone said, darkly. 'The council will have your guts for garters if we report this.'

'Or is it,' someone jabbed a finger at the monk, 'because he's a Buddhist?'

'You're all bloody mad,' the groundsman said, and he walked away. 'Barking bloody mad.'

We carried on playing as before and we never heard any more about it.

But on the occasions when I did take my turn in goal it was an opportunity for me to demonstrate the Scorpion Kick, the Handstand Save, the One-Handed Catch, the Tip-Over-The-Bar-With-Tongue and various other effortless tricks of a goalkeeper playing below his level.

So good was I in goal at this time, that I retired from football forever.

One of the Strollers who played in a regular Sunday league came to me needing a goalkeeper. (They always do.) Sunday morning football is a mighty institution in England and the municipal parks of the country do far better business than do its churches. In fact, it is a kind of religion. The football park is a place where the giant congregation of the chronically unskilled work off their Saturday night hangovers and crack their nicotine-varnished lungs in pursuit of hopelessly optimistic fantasies regarding their own footballing prowess. There are many denominations in our church: there is the confederation of cloggers; the league of lungers; the grand order of the out-of-position; the ministry of the missed-by-a-mile, all of whom march down to assemble on the green fields of municipal England every Sunday morning. The glorious and faithful brotherhood of the boot: fat blokes and lazy blokes; smoking blokes, and hungover and stoned blokes; married and unwed blokes; straight and gay blokes; thick and clever blokes; the working classes and the middle classes and the drinking classes. How can it be that such a gargantuan association goes so unreported and unrecorded? It's an institution bigger than the Church, but does it have representation in the House of Lords? It has more members than the Labour Party, but does it have a voice in government? Who is its spokesbloke on the TV? Where are its pressure groups? If it ever got organised, it would rule the country.

But it won't. It's not about that. Sunday football is about a million small dramas played out on a thousand muddy, mulchy municipal pitches, 100 yards by 60, the length and breadth of the country. Sunday football is where footballers go to die, happily, every week.

As I said, I'd given up this stuff after having developed a serious cartilage problem in my left knee. I couldn't afford private medicine and, like most of the rest of the country under Thatcherism, I was on a hospital waiting list that promised medical attention some time in the next decade. When I was approached to keep goal for this Sunday league team, my knee was stiff and swollen, but I thought that with a knee brace I'd probably be OK. I can't remember the name of the team I'd been asked to play for, but it was a pub team, based at the Old Bull on the south side of Leicester. Or was it the Olde Bell? Anyway, the opposition was Auto-Destruct Car Breaker's Yard United.

Yes.

I was asked to play because the regular goalie was injured. I got a ride to the ground in my Strollers friend's car, but on the way it was whispered to me that, if I performed well enough, I might have a regular spot. The regular keeps hadn't been doing too well and he'd been informed that the team were on the lookout for a new custodian.

I was a little alarmed to hear this. Thing is, I didn't remotely want a regular spot playing against thugs who couldn't control their emotions every time their own lack of skill was made manifest to themselves. I'd done all that and half the time it wasn't worth laundering the kit for. On this occasion, I'd only turned up to help out, but on my arrival in the dressing-room it began to seem like I was auditioning.

It was a home fixture, and since it was the home team's responsibility to provide a referee it turned out that the injured goalkeeper had been given the silver whistle. He came into the dressing-room as I pulled on my shirt. An athletic, bald-headed type, with red-rimmed eyes, he ground his knuckles into his hips, scowled at me and went out again.

'What was that about?'

'He thinks you want his place,' someone said, stamping his foot into a studded boot.

I looked around at my teammates. No one had eye

contact for me; they were busy pulling on socks, lacing up boots, slapping on the Deep Heat. I'd somehow been set up to audition for a part I had no interest in.

I strapped on my knee brace – that got me a bit of eye contact – and hoped to get through the game. It did make me look like one of those sad boys with a coin box – badly painted plaster mannequins of chronic polio victims or whatever – you used to see stationed outside department stores. The brace protected my knee by reducing lateral movement on the ligament. The downside of one of these things is that it tends to reduce lateral movement on you altogether, which isn't great for a goalkeeper. But as it happened, I might as well have not strapped it on at all, because the ref was out to get me.

Five minutes into the game, one of their players walked off the pitch to spit a great evil gob of tobacco and lung-tissue that the opening minutes had detached from his respiratory system. Someone from the opposition hoofed a long ball back into our half and, seeing it drop, the spittoon expert jogged back onto the field and picked up the ball, perhaps ten or even twelve yards offside. It was so far offside and such a blatant infringement that I simply thought he was being daft. I held out my hands for him to give me the ball and made no attempt to stop him when he dribbled round me and slotted the ball into the net. I mock-applauded him, but he was already running up the pitch, celebrating his 'goal'.

His teammates, too. The referee awarded the goal.

I wasn't having that. I walked up to baldy and, in a low voice, I said, 'What are you doing? Firstly, it's an infringement to go off the field and come on again without being signalled to do so. Secondly, he was offside by three miles.'

He gritted his teeth. 'I've no linesman to make fine judgements,' he said. 'The goal stands.'

There was nothing I could do. Everyone just wanted to get on with the game.

A few minutes later, the opposition mounted their first real attack. Their striker came through and I went out to meet him. He fired low, and I went down and collected the ball comfortably into my chest. The striker jumped over me (he was one of the decent ones who don't want to take off your head), but he caught the toe of his boot on my elbow.

Penalty.

I walked up to baldy again. 'You've got to be joking! You don't know what you're doing!'

'Get on with it!'

The penalty was slotted home. Two–nil.

A bit later the ref blew his whistle when he said I'd infringed the four-step rule. This bloody silly rule, fortunately obsolete now, dictated that goalkeepers should release the ball from their hands after four steps. It meant you could put it on the floor, dribble it to the edge of the area and then pick it up again. It was an impossible rule to enforce, which was why it was discarded. You might go up to catch a cross and your momentum as you came down with the ball might easily take you over four steps. No referee ever called you on it, unless it was a blatant and deliberate infringement.

Before half-time, a third goal had gone in, again yards offside by anybody's reckoning. I'd had enough. With the opposition celebrating, I marched up to baldy for a third time. 'Proved a point, have you? Got your place sorted for next week? Can we play football now?'

'Any more lip from you,' he said, 'and you're off for an early shower.'

'Listen, I don't want your fucking place in the team. I'm just here for the day.'

'I'm warning you.'

'Let it go, Graham,' I heard someone say from behind me.

I walked back to my goalmouth, but I was furious. Worse, it seemed I was the only person on the pitch who knew what was happening here. I felt the guy glaring at my every touch. I couldn't stay focused on the game. Every time I looked up, he'd be glowering at me, like a sorcerer trying to fix me with a hex. I let another two in; quite soft goals, as I remember. The whistle went at 5–0.

A few of the lads invited me to join them for a beer after the game. For Sunday league football, this is as much a part of the pleasure as the game. In fact, for many players it's more important than the game. It's when you get to unpick the match, replay a few moves and laugh about how crap you all are. We all went down to the Hanged Man or whatever the pub was called and shouted in the pints. But the mood became very damp when we were joined by our referee.

There was a free chair next to me. He pointedly put his pint down on the far side of the table and dragged the free chair away from me and over to his pint. There he sat in poisonous silence, sipping bitter ale and saying nothing.

'Another pint?' someone asked me.

'No,' I said. 'I'll have to be going.'

I got home and had a bath. My knee was swollen all over again and I'd collected a couple of bruises from Auto-Destruct Car Breaker's Yard United. I thought, bugger it, I'm too old for this. Bloody silly overgrown schoolboys, channelling their insecurity and anger and small dicks into a 90-minute yelling festival every weekend. I was 34 and I was ready to throw away my football boots.

After that ignominious game, I lay in the bath and thought that I should do something else with my time instead of watching football and playing football. Writing a novel, maybe.

Enough football.

Until, of course, some 15 years later, when that bloody Phil Oltermann got in touch with his sparky line about Nigel Spackman and I found that I was enjoying the event just as much as I had hated the game where that silly goalie was convinced I wanted his shirt.

I was having a good time again. The blue-shirted Italians were breaching the sea wall at every point, threatening the deluge, and I was having fun. My teammates had turned out to be a good bunch of lads and I'd done all right so far. I'd baffled the Italians' top scorer and I'd given someone's ear a bloody good tug. That was what goalkeeping was all about.

The psychology of goalkeeping is extraordinary and contoured. Look at the dimensions of the goal: it's an incredible eight yards wide by eight feet high. Pace that eight yards *indoors* – go on, do it now, this is important – to get a sense of what I'm talking about here. It's fucking massive! Eight yards! It's impossible to swing your leg at a ball and not put it through that sort of space. Talk about hitting a barn door. This is twice a barn door. How can anyone not score with that sort of target to aim at?

And there are times when you are goalkeeping and you've made a couple of saves, and you feel like your shoulders are brushing the bar and your elbows are rubbing the posts. You're a giant for a while. Then you make a schoolboy howler and suddenly the stewardship of that space seems intolerable. It's like guarding the door to an aircraft hangar.

Confidence in goalkeeping is everything. If you want to bugger up a young goalkeeper's confidence, just ask Steve McClaren, because he's a bloody expert.

It's 2007 and England need to beat Croatia at home to qualify for Euro 2008. The team have put themselves in a pressured situation. The two choice, experienced keepers – James and Robinson – have been wobbling lately. You have a capacity crowd at an intimidating stadium for a very tense fixture. The pitch is greasy. So, what do you do? You send on an untested young goalkeeper.

For God's sake! Talk about the Roman Colosseum.

It's easy to be wise afterwards. Well, I was wise before, and to prove it my wife remembers me howling at the TV set because she jumped and spilled her cup of tea all over her new frock. (What is a frock anyway? I'm glad she won't read this.) I thought it was lunacy. Carson was and is a fine goalkeeper. But this was the crucible. He was a rookie. This was his competitive international debut. Eight minutes into the game, Nico Kranjcar sends in a speculative shot from thirty yards out, not particularly threatening and something that Carson would normally deal with in a blink.

The ball goes through his hands. England fail to qualify.

It was a horror movie. McClaren was sacked the next day. It took Scott Carson at least a season to recover and get back to where he was.

Yes, Carson can be blamed. But the defence he had in front of him that night was awful too, and a keeper – experienced or not – is affected by the hive-mind of the team. England are still suffering from a goalkeeping crisis, but they are also suffering from a defensive crisis, a midfield crisis, a goalscoring crisis, a penalty-taking crisis, a management crisis, a dickheads-at-Lancaster Gate crisis, and they are all so deeply desperate and short of ideas that they have now recruited a brilliant Italian who doesn't even speak English to be the England manager. His lack of English seems to be helping.

But journalists do keep talking about this goalkeeping crisis in the England football team. For half a century, it was never an issue. The custodian was consistently solid, reliable and indisputably world class. There is an almost regal line that runs from Gordon Banks (1963–72), through Peter Shilton (1970–90) to David Seaman (1988–2002). Apart from a few stopgaps, try-outs and fill-ins, only the also brilliant young pretender Ray Clemence (1972–83) laid any real claim to rightful possession of the Gloves of Greatness. What happened?

There's never been a worse time to play in goal. The back-pass rule and the introduction of the ridiculous lightweight, swerving circus ball have put more pressure on goalies than ever. YouTube replays every blunder, and TV magnifies every rueful smile from the beaten keeper. Paul 'Air-Kick' Robinson and David 'Calamity' James get rubbished in the media in ways that seem cruelly designed to drag their confidence levels still lower. With so many foreign goalies guarding the Premiership sticks, beyond these two only a few promising but callow, untested youths remain. These feel like the wilderness years. We await the Return of the King.

Banks, Shilton and Seaman were, of course, all guilty of howlers; it's part of the narrative of goalkeeping and always has been. Robinson and James lack for nothing as goalkeepers but consistency and confident psychology. And no England team – no football team anywhere – is going to win anything unless the number 1 shirt is filled by a man with those attributes.

Our two best keepers right now are Paul Robinson and David James, no question. On his day, James is the better keeper, no question about that either. But it's not always his day, and Robinson beats him for consistency; or did, until recently.

What happened to make Paul Robinson go through a terrible dip in confidence and form? I mean apart from the media drubbing, which would undermine and topple a medieval fortress, let alone a human being. There's more to it than that.

A goalie and his back four have a special relationship. The keeper must impart confidence to his back four. If he does so, it will encourage them to play a higher line. This, in turn, enables the midfield to push on. This is often unconscious; when your keeper is shaky, you stay deeper than where your manager is screaming for you to play, because of an unconscious fear. The goalkeeper is the indicator of the team's unconscious mind.

But the keeper doesn't get his state of mind from a vacuum. The relationship is complementary. He must, in turn, draw confidence from the knowledge that he has a solid back line in front of him. Paul Robinson and David James for some time now have had to endure in front of them a ragged line-up of prima donnas, hopheads, dimwits, basket cases and *Hello!* magazine fashion shows. Just take a moment to examine the condition of the 'fortress' in front of the England goalkeeper in recent years.

Rio Ferdinand. Flaky on or off the pitch. I'm sorry, but claiming you forgot your professional footballer's drugs-test appointment is like claiming you can't remember which town you're from because it was dark when you left. We won't even mention the incident of kicking a Chelsea female ground steward after a lost game. When we were getting hammered by the Italians, we didn't try to remedy the matter by sticking the boot into the elderly Italian woman whose job it was to mop out the changing-rooms. And this is a guy who was considered for the captaincy of the national game!

The captain is not chosen because he's the best player. He's chosen because he's an admirable bloke: a model of masculinity in behaviour, deportment and spirit; a rock in the swirling waters of the game, which brings me to the current England captain.

John Terry. Much as you love his lionheart, he keeps going missing at international level. I don't mean dodging games or skipping drugs tests like Rio; I mean he's often caught out of position. But then again Terry is punchy from much-publicised binge-drinking, publicly naked vomiting sessions and regular nightclub brawling. And then there's the weeping over missing a penalty. My lad cried when he missed a penalty once. He was seven at the time. You can't have as a captain a man who cries and sucks his thumb, however big-hearted.

Gary Neville. Now, he's the kind of fighter you would want on any side, but he's got a psychotic perma-scowl that must frighten even his own grannie. Ask him what he thinks of having four at the back and he'll say, 'I can't stand Liverpool, I can't stand Liverpool people, I can't stand anything to do with them.' Ask him what he thinks of the Charity Shield and he'll say, 'I can't stand Liverpool, I can't stand Liverpool people, I can't stand anything to do with them.' In fact, when Rio got suspended for the drugs fiasco, Neville seriously wanted to organise a strike amongst his England teammates. Politics! Tremendous! I can just see him sitting down and penning a letter requesting solidarity from the Knitting, Footwear & Allied Trades Union. And God help us if we ever have a Scouse goalie playing for England.

Then there's *Ashley Cole*, a player who, when he's not posing for *Hello!* magazine, is likely to be having illicit behind-your-back meetings with another team. Here is a man who had to stop his car and be sick in the lay-by on hearing from his agent that Arsenal wouldn't pay him a penny over 60k *a week*. There was some sort of dispute over whether he or Arsenal should pay his agent's fees. (Footnote: if I make a deal through my agent for this book, I'm the one who pays the agent. The publisher doesn't pay the agent, and neither does the football team. It works like that for writers just as it does for footballers. That's how it's always worked.)

Did the England manager need five men at the back? Yes, he did. In addition to these four, he needed to pull in a shrink. I'm deadly serious. As a goalkeeper, it's no fun having flakes in front of you. Would you trust any of these men with your wallet, or to look after your infant child for half an hour? It's only football, you might say, but when you're playing at any level for 90 minutes, it's front-line trench warfare and you have to depend on teammates with the temperament to hold the line without a squeak.

Sven-Göran Eriksson rarely criticised his own players, but after a shocking defensive display against Sweden in the 2006 World Cup his loyalty and tact were tested to the limit. After the game, he was left mouthing off about how his defence kept going missing. 'We defended badly and we can't deny that,' he said. 'In the dressing-room, there is a board set out with the pitch drawn on it. It is written there which players they have to mark and all the positions they should stay in.'

It's not laziness or inability on the part of the players; it's lack of integrity that leads to the much-bemoaned 'loss of shape'. They won't stick to a plan. You can't depend on them. England's back four are hopelessly reactive. They don't have the confidence to get in an opponent's face, because they don't trust that there's someone there to back them up. The line wobbles, and Robinson and James always have to second-guess their own defence for every new wave of attack.

Compare David Seaman, with Tony Adams and Martin Keown in front of him. Or think of Mark Wright, Paul Parker and Stuart Pearce in Italia '90. Who would you prefer to have on your side in a scrap? Or strapped across your 18-yard line? Compare the psychology. It's not as if we don't have options at the back. There's Matthew Upson, Micah Richards, Jamie Carragher, Ledley King, Joleon Lescott, Leighton Baines, Wes Brown . . . Capello is on it, too.

You don't have to be a shrink to see that when England mend the back line, they will mend the goalkeeping problem.

OK, so I'm enjoying myself in Italy, but my confidence that we can do anything to hold back the surging tide is draining. Everyone knows we're knackered. We've been holding back the deluge on enthusiasm alone. But who cares? The Tuscan sky is still blue. The plastic pitch is still green. A great day to be a middle-aged footballer at, ahem, international level.

Early in the first half, one of my boys gives away a free-kick just outside the box, five yards off the 'D'. It was a foul, but more a tired-leg swing arriving late than anything deliberate. It certainly didn't require the Italian striker to shriek, fling himself to the ground and roll across the pitch in an operatic simulation of ceremonial beheading because the ref was always going to give the free-kick.

That's OK. It gives me the chance to make a wall. At non-professional level, they have to be bloody good to bend the ball around the wall.

Making a wall should be a simple thing. Somehow, it's not. Playing for England Writers, we keep running into trouble, even just building this wall.

Properly setting up the wall in a *timely* manner will usually be the difference between success and failure for the defending team. It should be easy. I have an intelligent set of players in front of me: putatively intelligent, writers of distinction. But they get so distracted by the threat of the quickly taken kick that they forget to be directed by their goalkeeper. And it's the goalie's job to set the wall. My job.

Now, let's examine this task.

The wall is called a wall because it is designed to do what all walls are made to do: to stop things from passing through them. In this case, it should stop the struck ball from travelling towards the goal. (I know this sounds blindingly obvious, but you'll have to forgive me. I'm talking to my mates in my team when I say: try kicking a ball yourself against a real brick wall, notice that it doesn't pass through it; then try kicking it at the wall a second time until the significance of this is clear to you. Go on, strike it really hard. It still doesn't get through.)

Anyway, the first thing that has to happen is that the keeper determines whether a wall is necessary. The only person who can make this decision is the keeper since it's the keeper who is ultimately responsible for the result of the free-kick. Once the keeper has determined a wall is necessary, the next thing that the keeper must do is determine how many players it needs to construct the wall. There isn't a set number of players because it depends upon many factors, including range, position, etc. Each keeper might have a different preference towards numbers in a given situation, so it's something that the keeper must articulate quickly and clearly. One way in which this is done is for the keeper to yell, 'TWO!' or 'THREE!' If the outfield players are somewhat slow-witted, it helps to hold up the number of fingers corresponding to the number yelled.

The kick was quite close to the penalty box, so I'm yelling, 'FOUR! FOUR!' and holding up four fingers. Trouble is, only two players have heard me. So, I start bellowing at certain individuals to get across and line up in the wall. Whereupon others take it upon themselves to join the wall, so now I seem to have a wall of six or seven players in front of me. This just gets me even more annoyed: the Italians might not choose to take a direct shot and now three of them are lined up on the other side of the box ready to latch onto a neat cross as an alternative. So, I start bellowing names to get out of the wall, then five of them decide to split off from the wall, leaving two again.

Now, I'm swearing at my own players to get another

two back in the wall. I can feel myself going purple in the face, as I shred my own larynx. One of the other players trots back and takes up position on a post, like you do for a corner. This is completely fucking useless since it only plays onside the Italian forwards close to the goal. I give him a bollocking and send him back to the wall, all the time trying to keep my eye on the ref and the ball in case of a snapshot before we've finished our ridiculous square dance. (I've never forgotten that last international at the old Wembley stadium. England's goalkeeper David Seaman was still trying to arrange his defensive wall when German Dietmar Hamann took a quick free-kick. Seaman couldn't keep it out and the Hun had beaten England 1–0.) Anyway, I finally get my four lined up. I'm exhausted from the effort of doing that alone, but at least we've got it sorted. Kind of.

When you've ultimately got the correct people in the wall – and it really shouldn't be this hard – it's up to you, the keeper, to set them up quickly. The easiest way to do this is for the keeper to go to the near post and work on positioning with the number-one player in your wall. If the number-one player is correctly positioned, numbers two, three and four rally to number-one's side. At the moment, for some inexplicable reason, my two, three and four players are stepping left and right, forward and backward, and shaking their tushes like showgirls in a Pigalle nightclub.

What? What? Just make a wall!

I'm roaring for them to close up because this behaviour tends to leave an interstice in the wall through which the ball can mysteriously pass unimpeded. Did you like all that writers' clever double-talk about interstices and mystery? It's a hole! There are fucking big holes in the wall! God help me!

Don't forget the opposition are placing the ball at this moment and deciding who is going to thwack it. Luckily for us, they're trying on a ridiculously complicated three-way possibility of a run from left, right and straight on. They've watched too much soccer on TV. Thankfully, they are as inept at this sort of thing as we are.

There are different methods for the keeper and key wall-player one to communicate. Having player one turn and face the keeper is good, because in the hurly-burly that is modern writers' league football, the number-one player can't see that the enraged keeper is by now like a dog with rabies and gnawing his near post.

I'm bellowing to Conrad Williams to turn and look at me, so I can wave him into position and he in turn can drag Nick, Phil and Tim into covering the angle I want blocked. Finally, he turns, sees me waving him over and steps to the left. Good. He reaches to pull Nick across, who goes with him, while Tim and Phil mysteriously step to the right. I'm apoplectic now. Honestly, I'm shredding my own gloves with my teeth. I'm going to need counselling after this.

As you can see, the proper use of a wall requires thought, planning, quick teamwork and only a modest IQ. This is a great example of how the people who say you have to be crazy to be a keeper are so wrong. The truth is you have to be clever and patient and charming – yes! – to get things organised and set up so quickly. It's no good bellowing at your team after the Italian Writers' XI have struck the back of the net and are squealing *Si! Si Si!* like excitable piglets having their testicles sucked by the callused mouth of a farmer from the eastern Dolomites, is it? No.

So, seeing the gap in the wall, the right-positioned Italian striker runs at the ball and steps over it. My useless wall instantly fragments and dances right. The left-positioned Italian striker runs at the ball and steps over it. My useless wall splinters and steps left. The centrally positioned striker runs at the ball and, with a clear and unimpeded view of the goal, blasts it about 30 feet above the bar.

'That's not a wall,' I mutter quietly to myself, sadly.

I swear to you I love my Writers' XI teammates like brothers, but sometimes they exasperate me when all I want them to do is stand upright in front of the goal and hang onto their dear bollocks.

Anything can catch you out when you are a goalie. Anything. Just like in real life. In fact, goalkeeping is real life to the square power of 44. You can get caught out by being too good, by knowing too much, just like David Seaman against Brazil.

When I was growing up in the '60s near the pit where my dad worked, contractors started building a huge installation right next to it. We used to climb over the fence and play amid all the plant equipment, and try not to get caught. What they were building was a smokeless-fuel processing plant that would take the raw coal and make it into smokeless Homefire nuggets. These nuggets were called Bronowski's Bricks, after Jacob Bronowski, the genius who developed the process. (Bronowski was certainly a genius. A polymath who was fascinated equally by the arts and the sciences, he wrote and narrated the popular TV series *The Ascent of Man*, which was also published in book form. This would have qualified him to play for our football team.)

Bronowski was hired by the National Coal Board to preside over the design of this industrial process. It made sense to build the plant next to a deep mine to eliminate transport costs. But when the industrial plant was up and running, the coal from our pit was found to be too brittle: it broke, and when it broke it clogged up the works. They had to transport anthracite all the way from the Welsh valleys to feed through the processor. A brilliant concept, a massive design, but all undone by one small oversight. This has always struck me as an illustration of how too much cleverness can leave you looking stupid. Which is why I'm boring you with the story now.

So, where was I? David Seaman, that's right. Seaman ended a truly brilliant career for England with an error that was actually caused not by his shortcomings as a goalkeeper but the very opposite. (He had a bloody silly and annoying ponytail, too, but that didn't contribute to his downfall. Much.)

It's England v. Brazil in the World Cup quarter-finals. Seaman, a brilliant shot-stopper and as good as any in a one-on-one, has had a good competition. So have the England team as a whole. Don't hold your breath, but they're looking like they have a pretty good chance of making the final . . . if they can just step past the mighty Brazil. England take the lead, then Brazil steal an equaliser. The game is poised when Brazil get a free-kick on the touchline, oh, fully 40 yards out. Ronaldinho takes it.

Seaman sees Ronaldinho set himself for the kick; he sees Ronaldinho shape his body; he knows that not even the superb Ronaldinho is going to try to score from there, because it would be a wasted free-kick. It's like plucking cherries from a tree for someone of Seaman's ability. Anticipating the trajectory of the cross, Seaman is off his line and advancing at the moment the ball is struck. He can do this because he is expert, confident and accomplished at reading the flight of the ball early. That's what great keepers do.

The ball loops and swerves away from the Brazilian attack line. With a kind of mounting horror, Seaman realises he's advanced too far. He back-pedals furiously. The ball dips, swerves and bizarrely ends up in the back of the net.

It's a fluke, a freak, but Ronaldinho will claim he intended it. It's a lie.

This sort of goal is not all that uncommon; you've seen it many times before, the mis-hit cross that drops in the net. The goalscorer always claims he intended it, but in reality it's just a cross that goes awry. And that's what this is.

Since Ronaldinho is a soccer genius, he somehow gets away with his outrageous claim that he intended this as a shot, and because he's a magnificent footballer some people believe him. Well, Ronaldinho *is* a magnificent footballer, but he's not a conjurer. He doesn't have occult powers over the ball. If Seaman had been a lesser goalkeeper, he would have saved it easily. He was undone by his own confidence, ability and goalkeeping prescience, which on this crucial occasion let him down.

You cannot legislate for the fluke. England went out of the competition and Seaman openly wept. He never entirely recovered. He played a few more games for England, but the end of his 14 years as national custodian – a decade of it unchallenged – can be dated back to that moment.

Christ, we were all glad when he had that ponytail cut off at a charity event.

Fifteen minutes into the second half, lungs cracking, legs gone, we fold. (Is it because I know my teammates might read this that I understate?) They are puce in the face, their muscles have turned to slush, they are hyperventilating and they are making lunging tackles that leave them on the floor and the opposition still with the ball. You get the picture. It's all right for me to mock – I'm standing between the sticks and I'm not the one whose lungs are cracking. The Italians are playing simple balls through the channels, and now they slot a goal home. And another. And another.

Not Francesco, though. He just can't seem to poke one in.

The most agonising of the goals that go past me is the last. Tim Adams, who wrote a great book about tennis star John McEnroe, has been – and he won't thank me for reporting this – a tower of strength at the back and has run himself into the ground. One of those stiletto-like through-balls is slipped between our midfielders, and Tim is in a race for it against one of their strikers. Luckily, Tim has three yards' advantage, with the ball between him and me. I call to him to roll it back to me, so I can clear it upfield. Then I see in Tim's face that he's not going to make it. I mean he's done. The engines have shut down. He can't get any more breath in his lungs and his limbs are oxygen-starved. His face is registering all this – which is to say that although his body is shutting down, his brain is recording the moment with rising horror.

'Just toe it! Just toe it!' I yell at him. By which I mean all he has to do is stretch out a toe to nudge it back to me and I can put it in row Z in the empty stands. An expression crosses his face that I've seen before somewhere. It's in that film *Zulu* in the close-up of a red-coated soldier in a pith helmet, then the camera pulls back to reveal that he has taken a spear full in the midriff. It's also in *Star Wars*, when some guy has had his head scythed by a light sabre and it hasn't yet toppled off his neck, but it will any second. You get the idea. This is the expression on Tim's face as he tries but fails to stretch out a toe in front of him. Then he falls over.

Gleeful Italian striker nips round Tim's prone body, collects the ball, advances towards me – bang! It's Italy 5, England 1. Goodnight, Florence. Time for bed, said Zebedee.

There's no blame on Tim, who has flogged his guts for us and put in a better performance than I have. It's just a good example of what happens when a bunch of middle-aged writers indulge the fantasy that they were once and still could be athletes. And the sick thing about it? It's that the Italian writers seem to think this victory has something to do with their skills, rather than our crapness.

The whistle blows. It's our very first game as England Writers' XI and we've been put to the sword. And you want to know the great thing about maturity? Two minutes after the final whistle it doesn't hurt at all.

It's an interesting thing, but people off the pitch can be very different from who they are on the pitch. As I mentioned before, it's not like your true character comes out in a game; it's more complicated than that. It's not like there is one compressed personality waiting to be revealed while playing football or under any other stressful conditions. On the contrary, you see that human beings are variable creatures, pushed by extreme pressure (I know it's about having fun, but, still, a game of football is a species of extreme pressure) into a diversity of shapes and turns of temperament.

Our Italian hosts, who had been pulling our shirts and arguing over every throw-in, were delightful, warm, generous hosts in Florence. The only thing I have against them is that they organised a dreadful cultural evening for us all to attend, probably to justify the enormity of the spectacle of crap footballers on a sponsored junket. Representatives of each national team were called upon to discuss issues of literary interest and, even worse, read some of their work. In Swedish, for example. Or translated into Italian from the original Swedish, with both versions being read aloud. Just so you don't think I'm being narrow about this, my heart went out to the non-English-speaking Hungarian team, who, cigarette-less in the auditorium, blinked patiently through the occasional brief translations into English, which was designated the 'second language' of the programme. I observed that a Hungarian blink can sometimes last a very long time.

The event somehow filled the evening from 7 p.m. until midnight – I can't imagine Wayne Rooney standing for that – but you could sneak out and refill your wine glass, and outside in the hall you would find some of the Italian team.

'Hey, Paolo and Stefano, shouldn't you be inside, listening to the cultural event?' Paolo and Stefano made praying motions, hoping the literary part of the evening would end soon.

Those with whom we had locked horns earlier in the afternoon we now befriended. The Swedes too, buoyant at the manifestation of free alcohol, were bristling after having beaten the Hungarians 3–0. Their early success and the Tuscan Vimto had made them garrulous and confident.

One of the Italians took the wine glass out of my hand and led me to a table of superior stuff – also sponsored – and insisted that I try it. 'Better,' he said. I agreed. Then he said, 'Hey, today you *pull-a* my ear!'

I hadn't realised who it was. A football kit makes people look taller on the pitch.

'Oh, that. Yes.'

We were joined by one of his teammates, who was interested in what we were talking about.

'Why? Why you *pull-a* my ear?'

I didn't know what to tell him. 'It's an English thing,' I heard myself saying, just making it up. As usual.

'Oh!' said the newcomer. 'He told me you pull his ear! Yes, I heard about this. It's like a warning, *si*?'

'Yes,' I said doubtfully.

He turned to his friend. 'I told you. It's an English warning.'

'An English warning?'

'*Si*. It was in Shakespeare.' He turned to me and smiled. 'That's very English.'

'It is?' I said. I've never seen it in no Shakespeare. Bite your thumb at me, sir, but not pull his ear.

'Oh, yes. Very English.'

For the rest of the competition, some members of the Italian team would look at me and waggle their ear. They'd bought my story. Either that or it's an Italian gesture for 'Fuck off, you ugly, English, big-nosed prat.' Anyway, now a generation of Italian writers think that having your ear grabbed is an Englishman's fun way of saying *watch out*.

One by one, the writers were sneaking out of the dire readings and socialising in the corridors. I don't know why a Hungarian has to pretend to understand a word of a Swedish poem translated into Italian, or vice versa, in order to justify a game of football, but I guess these were the miraculous and barely credible terms on which we were there.

Tomorrow we would be able to stop this nonsense and get back to football, as we lined up against the Magyars.

Despite the 5–1 drubbing, the English team were all in pretty high spirits. Letting in five goals doesn't look great for goalkeepers, but the one-sidedness of the result tends to exonerate us. It's quite possible to play well and still get beaten by such a margin. You'll have had more work to do and presumably you managed to save some of the things that were thrown at you. At least no one in the team seemed to be blaming me for the result.

Blame – in either direction – is interesting, from a keeper's point of view. Yes, Schmeichel would scream at his defence if the opposition ever even got a shot in, and there is always a brief and pointless moment after you've conceded a goal when you stare back at the weak spot in your defence. But there's no sense in shouting or moaning, because they know. They already know. Your defenders know if they've let a man get past them, or failed to get in a challenge, or fell down on the job, or simply stood off. It's just something that doesn't need analysing or pointing out.

Similarly, you know yourself if you made a poor fist of it. Your own defenders never rail at you. An instant of eye contact is enough to tell you that they know you know. On the rare occasion that it does happen, it will come from the character who can do no wrong himself but who pathologically needs to apportion blame elsewhere. The presence of that kind of whining and moaning psychology can thoroughly demotivate a team, unless that person is a superlative footballer indeed. You can only take it from someone who is very, very good. I imagine Roy Keane to have been that kind of individual. But you'd have to have his brilliance and work rate to get away with moaning on such a monumental scale.

I know my weaknesses as a keeper (if not always in life) and they are manifest. I know when to hold up my careless hands, and will do so when I've made a mistake but not when it's down to another player who wants to have a go at me for his own shortcomings.

Once, while playing for my college, we were up against some university team on a cold, rainy windswept afternoon. In a tight and scoreless game under a dark sky, the opposition won a free-kick just outside the box and I lined up an orthodox four-man wall in front of me.

The kick was taken, a hard drive at grass level. For some reason, my central defender in the wall lifted his foot and let the ball shoot underneath. I was on the other side of the goal and couldn't get to it. The guy who'd lifted his foot turned and glowered at me – actually bared his teeth.

As I say, blame is neither useful nor necessary in football. *The goal has gone in. Get on with trying to win one back.* But some people can't help themselves. On this occasion, I must have felt provoked by the ugly curl of my teammate's twisted lip. I knew who was in the wrong, so I got eyeball to eyeball with him and bared my teeth right back in his face. We were like two nasty dogs in a pit ring. Someone much more sensible than either of us shouted, 'Leave it.'

Afterwards we had a laugh about it – in the way you pretend to laugh about these things.

It's a bit of a drag actually, that Albert Camus was a goalkeeper. Because of that one existentialist writer-goalkeeper, I feel like I've spent half my life tut-tutting at some analysis or another of the goalkeeping mentality that talks about us being outsiders and symbolic of alienation. What a load of cock!

One flaming existentialist! I've heard that Nabokov was a goalie, too. Does that mean that all goalkeepers are paedophiles hiding behind irony? Goalkeepers are not alienated existentialists; they're mostly too stolid to be anything other than what they are. I'm tempted to say *thick*. I'm tempted to say, *That's it, we're thick. Goalies are thick and we like it, duh.* But the word stolid is better and has it about right.

Banks, Shilton, Seaman, Schmeichel: all the goalies I've named as worthy of the title of greatness are not complex, brooding outsiders. Banks always stood in goal with a posture suggesting he was having a quick smoke, waiting until someone gave him the nod to deliver the next 14 bags of coal. Shilton couldn't wait to get showered and rush down the bookies. All television reporters could ever get out of Seaman was a pleasing but vapid chuckle. And Schmeichel proved he has no imagination whatsoever by agreeing to appear on *Strictly Come Dancing*. (Quick feet? No.)

Too much imagination is bad for a keeper. I could have been decent in goal were it not for the fact that I have too much imagination. That and I had a paper round.

Take penalties, for instance. It's like a visit to the hall of mirrors. It's a mind game trying to guess which side of the goal the spot-kicker is going to place the ball.

Though I hesitate to inscribe this one into the Book of Old Tricks, there is one genuine tip-off as to whether the penalty kicker is going to place the ball to your right or to your left, if you can make it work for you. There are certain problems inherent in that 1) professionals all know about this and, 2) non-professionals and even professionals under pressure are just as likely to unintentionally blast the ball straight down the middle, thus the goalkeeper who simply stands his ground has got statistically just as much chance of saving the penalty as the one who flings himself right or left. But who cares about statistics? It's skill, psychology, inspiration and drama we want, not statistics. So, when the spot-kicker places the ball, if he is right-footed, watch where his left foot is pointing. That's where the ball is going. It's not possible for the other foot to point any other way at the moment the ball is kicked.

Now, of course, a disciplined footballer is going to disguise all these hints-and-tells and is going to shape his body to deceive you, so you have to look for the unconscious tell. You do this by not being in the goalmouth when the penalty kicker places the ball on the spot. What a keeper needs to do is stand at the side of the goal and appear not to be watching. Fiddle with your goalie gloves, swig some water, smoke a pipe. But in those moments before he's set himself for the shot the spot-kicker will unconsciously point his left foot (or right foot, if he's a left-footed player) at the side where he intends the ball to go. I've used this bit of crucial goalkeeping psychology for some time. I expect it to pay off Real Soon Now.

Of course, it helps, too, if you're a halfway decent keeper. Knowing which way the ball is heading is one thing; getting to it is another, especially if a penalty is placed low and hard, and just inside the upright. You might just as well try to catch a bullet between your teeth.

It really is supposed to be the case – statistically – that if you just stand your ground for a penalty, most spot-kickers under pressure will blast the ball down the middle, or close enough to the goalkeeper for a save to be likely. If you make the full-length dive, you've probably blown it. So, I guess you should play the numbers: stand up strong, don't bother diving right or left, and you'll stop six out of ten shots. But you can't. Get that Albert Camus fruitcake to come here and explain why you can't.

You're in the moment of the penalty and it seems a denial of life itself to say that there is a six-in-ten chance it will go straight down your throat. If you stand upright and appear to make little effort, then your teammates (and the crowd, if you're a professional) are going to be less than impressed. So, to hell with the maths. Football, after all, is related to theatre.

Statistics just screw up your head anyway. Someone once told me that – mathematically – if a spun coin has fallen heads ten times in succession, the next throw still has a 50–50 chance of falling as a head. Yeah, maths. A minus times a minus is a plus. So, why can't I multiply my overdraft at the bank with my friend's overdraft and make money? (We have the brilliant mathematician Marcus du Sautoy – who has written books popularising maths – on our team and he's explained it to me, but I fear we have a long way to go.) You see there are mathematical statistics and there is real life. Six in ten? There's a penalty and I'm committed to stopping it.

'Just stand up straight, OK?'

It's a Greek guy, on the island of Crete. I'm somehow playing for a Greek team and it's all a big mistake. The score is 1–1, and the opposition has a penalty with three minutes to go. I don't even know how I came to be playing. Well, I do. It was a misunderstanding, as was most of my time in Greece.

In 1988, I quit my job in youth work, married my then girlfriend and went to live on a Greek island, so that I could concentrate on writing a novel. After a few wonderful months on Lesvos, living in a beach shack with no electricity, water from a pump and scorpions in the cracks of the walls, we moved to Crete for the winter. By this time, our Greek was so-so but trying to use it seemed only to generate multiple misunderstandings. (I've since found that even if you speak the language flawlessly, Greece is the place to go if you actually want multiple misunderstandings. Greeks are proud of their misunderstandings.)

On Lesvos, the only way to get mail was through the poste restante at the local post office. Gossip had told the postmaster that I was a writer. He looked at my name and concluded that I was a certain famous Irish writer.

When I went in for my post, he called me to the side and whispered that he'd discovered my identity (not that I'd ever made it a secret). After a while, I realised he was talking about James Joyce. I didn't know the Greek for 'long-since pushing up daisies', and the more I protested, the more he thought that I was desperate for anonymity and assured me that it would be a secret between us.

Some secret. Every time we walked into the local taverna he seemed to be there with his extended family, whereupon with a word from him the table would all rise and solemnly toast me: 'To James Joyce, the great writer.'

'What have you said now?' my wife wanted to know, cheeks flaming.

'Nothing!' I protested.

I had to go through this ritual for the rest of my stay on Lesvos. They used to send over bottles of wine, and it did occur to me that if they ever found out the truth I might be lynched.

Anyway, a similar thing happened in Crete. I lived in a beach house near Chania, and while out having a stroll one day I saw two or three waiters from a hotel enjoying a kickaround on the sand. I joined in, and naturally went in goal. It was all good fun. They asked me where I was from. Coventry, I said. In faltering Greek, I told them the Sky Blues had recently won the FA Cup final against Spurs. Yes, they'd heard of the club. One of them had watched the final on TV. He seemed very excited by something he'd seen on TV. He looked at me with what I thought to be excessive admiration for simply being a Coventry City fan.

The waiters were going to play again on Wednesday, they told me. There would be a few more people. Did I want to join them?

'Where?' I asked.

'*Etho*. Here,' they said. 'Right here. *Exi hores*. Six o' clock.'

Well, that sounded fun – a game on the beach. I said I'd be there and we parted happily.

I turned up in my trainers at the appointed time, surprised that there was only one of the waiters there. Where were the others? '*Apo etho*,' he said. 'This way.' He led me to a car and held the door open for me to get in.

'Where are we going?' I asked. 'I thought we were playing football.'

'*Ne, ne, viveus*. Yes, of course, football.' He drove up over the mountain and down the other side. The car journey lasted over an hour. 'Where are your boots?'

'I don't have them.'

'You don't have? We must get for you the boots!'

'What, to play on sand?'

'Sand?'

He drew up at a full-size stadium. I got out of the car still slightly bewildered. I think you know where this story is going. Somehow I had become a former goalkeeper of Coventry City who had played in the FA Cup final. On TV. I'd been brought in as a ringer. They quickly produced kit and boots for me.

The thing is I couldn't see how to pull myself out of it. You see people in films in these situations and you think, *Why don't you just explain?* But every attempt was brushed off as some excuse by me to pull out, which, of course, it was, but not for the reasons they were thinking. Plus we'd come a long way and I had no idea of where I was or how to get back. My only option was to go through with it.

The stadium was pretty much empty, but it was a serious game, with smart officials in full regalia. At the warm-up, those boys were lashing in their shots at pace, and I felt out of my depth before the kick-off. I thought: just hang in there, it's only 90 minutes.

Luckily, I caught a couple of flighted balls in the early exchanges and the opposition seemed to decide to keep the ball on the deck. They pretty much failed to break through a solid line in front of me and I didn't have all that much to do. I let one in from a corner, but we equalised almost immediately. It was one of those games, luckily for me, where, as a goalie, I was never really called to account. The score stayed level until three minutes to go, when we conceded a penalty.

'Just stand up. Don't dive,' said the guy who had driven me to the stadium. 'He will shoot it straight at you. This I know.'

I should have said: *I'm sorry, I'm a goalkeeper, I can't do that. It's against my religion. Existentialism and all that. Albert Thingy. Camus. There is only one penalty, and that's the penalty of the moment.* But my Greek wasn't up to it.

The opposition striker placed the ball and looked me in the eye. He glanced to my right. He glanced to my left. He sniffed hard. He bent down and re-spotted the ball. He shaped his hips to the right. Then he reshaped his hips to the left. Then he repositioned the ball a second time. *I've got you*, I said to myself. *I know where you're going*. What's more, I'm Steve Ogrizovic, Coventry's loyal servant, who more than any other single player kept the Sky Blues afloat in the Premiership for so long.

The player walked back and stood like a rugby kicker. He shaped right and that's where I went, diving long and low, arms fully extended. The ball went straight down the middle.

All the way back, the waiter who had recruited me told me: 'Goalkeepers must stand up for the penalty. Stand up!'

All the way back to Chania.

All the sodding way.

Following the 5–1 thumping from Italy, we face Hungary. They have a different physical look to them. Pale-faced, chain-smoking eastern Europeans with impressive moustaches and a melancholia that also sits bravely on the upper lip. They line up, and blink in the Florentine sunlight as if they've just been dragged from a cave. We do the national anthem thing, Nick Royle vocalising lustily again on behalf of us all. Then we shake hands and they present us each with a small bottle of, well, something. There is a medicinal red cross on the front label.

For this consideration, much thanks.

Since I'm the goalie, every player on the team gives me his bottle of, well, something, to 'look after'. They're all secretly hoping that I'll lose the bloody awful gunk. (It's herb bitters, I decide.) When you're goalie, you often get asked to take care of teammates' watches, wallets, keys and the like that they don't trust to the dressing-room. I have a noncey little bag for my gloves, hat, lipstick and the rest, so they all go in there.

Once when I was playing for the Olde Bell, or whatever it was, I had my bag nicked, with half the team's stuff in it. I have a pretty shrewd idea of who took it and when. There were a couple of kids on bikes, hanging round near the goals. They waited until I ventured out of my penalty area to make a clearance. Simple, really. Anyway, today at the stadium there are no kids on bikes, so the dozen or so bottles of Magyar glak look pretty safe.

(I'm not sure why the Hungarians handed us medicinal bitters that day, though maybe it wasn't such a bad idea. A year or two after these events, when we played in Israel, it would have come in very handy. By that time, we had been bolstered by former Subbuteo supremo Daniel Tatarsky, Old Etonian Musa Okwonga [author of *A Cultured Left Foot*] and novelists Joe Dunthorne and Jeremy Gavron. It was a three-way tournament between the Israelis, Germany and England, all expenses paid. Oh.

'I don't know, Dad. I think it's offered in atonement for the concentration camps and all that.'

'What?'

'Spirit of peace and reconciliation.'

'You bloody what?'

Right. The driver of the England team bus was a former goalkeeper of Beitar Jerusalem FC and a retired undercover cop. He berated me for wearing goalkeeper gloves, as if it was cheating. The Germans had brought in a couple of ringers [here we go again], including one who used to play professionally for Bayer Leverkusen in the Bundesliga. I was three feet away from him when he elbowed Marcus du Sautoy as they raced together for a ball, breaking a bone in Marcus's hand. It cut up rough out there, and we could have done with the Hungarian glak. Three Germans and one English player were hospitalised. Another German spent half the game sobbing on the side of the pitch.

The concept of football as a medium of peace and reconciliation is going to need some fine-tuning.)

Where was I? Ah, yes, the Hungarians, and our team's second glorious international fixture. National anthems, pennants, splendid team photographs, all that. I needn't bore you with the details of the game. Yes, I will: we lost 2–0. A more respectable scoreline, at least.

There are times as a goalkeeper when your training and habits go against you. A Hungarian right-winger, nippy as a hay cart under a full load, advances to the byline at the edge of the six-yard box and drives in a hard cross along the grass. I should just belt it into touch, but it goes against the orthodox creed that says you get down and gather it up with your hands. But if it's fast and low, it's hard to hold. I get down all right, but I parry it instead of holding the ball and the rebound goes to a Hungarian striker who, overexcited, slices it. It spins up in the air and drops over everyone's head into the net. A crap goal from a comedy of errors. I should have trusted my instincts and not my training and swung a foot at the ball instead.

The Hungarian team appear to have only one squad member who can speak good English. It kind of annoys me that he happens to be the player who scores this crap goal. He'd given a reading the previous night, the content of which had caused a minor difference of opinion in the England camp. The bloke in question had described probing a bullet-marked monument as a kind of Braille. Very poetic, I thought, but inaccurate because Braille is a system of raised dots, not holes. Convex, not concave. I happen to mention this in passing to one of my teammates, who thought I was being a bit pedantic.

I don't know about that. I don't really do pedantic. So I wiped my mouth on my sleeve and expressed the view that it doesn't matter how effing poetic the writing is, it still has to work in the real world. Some of the team agreed with me, some not. (Christ, you can tell how bored we were.) Here's how it lined up. Those in favour of things working in the real world: the genre writers, the children's writers, the journalists. Those against: the 'literary' writers. So that's it, then. It's official. High-minded Booker Prize-type literature is allowed to be inexact, erroneous and plain wrong.

What's more, from a goalkeeper's point of view, letting any poet put a goal past you is shameful; letting a bad poet slot one in is just unbearable. (Just for the record, I don't really hate all poets, just some of them. Matthew Hollis is a poet in our squad and a decent footballer, and a very fine chap he is, and I hope he'll write a nice cover quote when I get my anthology of verse published Real Soon Now.) My objection to poets is that they are very much in love with their own misery. And the terrible, awful realisation dawns on me that maybe goalkeepers are, too.

Is it possible to be a goalkeeper and have fun? 'Higuita!!' I want to shout. Viva Higuita!!

The most barmy goalkeeper in the world was René Higuita. A complete loon. In a 1995 international against England, the Colombian goalkeeper astonished everyone by what he called his 'scorpion kick'. Jamie Redknapp had lobbed the ball towards the Colombian goalmouth. It was about head height and on target for the goal: useless as the cross it was meant to be and a simple catch for the goalkeeper?

No.

Higuita, who looked like a spliff-toking refugee from a Cheech and Chong stoner video, spread his arms wide and leapt forward in a true superhero flight, bringing his feet up behind him and successfully clearing the ball, apparently with either his heels or the undersides of his boots. This only 20 minutes into the game. With the score at 0–0. In an international fixture. At Wembley.

Afterwards, he said, 'I like to enjoy myself.'

Of course, if he'd mistimed this jaw-dropping stunt, he'd have been the clown goalkeeper until the end of days. As it is, he cleared the ball and is still the clown goalkeeper until the end of days. It's the most wonderful, spectacular and utterly stupid save ever recorded. Why catch the ball when you could do that?

Higuita was born and raised in poverty. Professional football in Colombia, just like in the UK and everywhere else now, is dominated by business. Local business in Medellín was cocaine. They've never actually had the word printed on the football shirts of the teams they sponsor, but that's where the money came from. *Tonight's big match, brought to you by Cocaine, Inc.*

So, your boss, the one that likes to be seen with soccer heroes, the one who buys your drinks and puts his arm around you after a good game, is the drugs-cartel chief Pablo Escobar. Higuita was quite open about their personal friendship. While Escobar is portrayed in the West as the evil drugs baron, red in tooth and claw, in Medellín he was always regarded as something of a local hero, bringing jobs and prosperity to an impoverished corner of the world.

When Higuita visited Escobar in prison, the world press went hoopla. Then, in the mid-'90s, Higuita got involved in a kidnapping case, having offered his mediating services to ensure the safe return of a kidnapped girl. Higuita was rewarded with cash, but since Colombian law outlaws involvement of any sort in such transactions, Higuita spent seven months in the slammer.

'I'm a footballer,' he said. 'I don't know anything about kidnapping laws.' René, on this occasion, you tried to catch it when you should have just punched it clear.

So, he misses the 1994 World Cup, and the next year he comes to the hallowed Wembley turf, where he thinks: life is short and too dull to make an ordinary catch. One day you're in prison, one day you're at Wembley stadium. Have fun.

And it is all great fun, but the fact is, his eccentric style and his sense of play caused him to let in several goals for his national side. He was a bloody idiot, a prankster who insulted the essential seriousness of the game. But in a drab, stale 0–0 yawn with England, he alone was worth the ticket money. Praise Higuita! Praise him!

'I like to enjoy myself.'

Enjoyment? Isn't that what makes football the most popular sport in the entire world? Why schoolboys – and lately plenty of schoolgirls – can't wait to fill their breaktimes and lunchtimes kicking a ball around in the school yard? Isn't enjoyment what it was always supposed to be about?

I like playing *Dads & Lads* on Knighton Park in Leicester. Kids need fresh air. It's scientifically documented that children who go outside more often do better at school. Bright kids do better and thick kids do better. Disruptive kids do better and so do well-behaved kids. And so do autistic kids, come to that. Yes, a kid who kicks a ball around will improve his or her school performance because of the superior oxygen that feeds his or her brain.

So, how come the parks aren't crowded out with Dads playing with their Lads? Quite apart from the question of their school performance, boys adore it. They adore being with their dads in a context of play. They love it because they know they are learning about football and about life all at the very same time. They are watching for cues on what it is to be a man. Dads are models of how to be grown up.

My boy Joe and I are lucky to have found a great bunch of *Dads & Lads* to play with. I've talked with the dads and we've agreed that you end up doing more parenting in an hour or so of *Dads & Lads* than in an entire week. The boys are intensely emotional; incredibly moody. There are always issues of fair play. They grow visibly when they've done something well; they collapse when things go against them. (The boys in question are all nine or thereabouts, a tricky age. There's a big difference between a nine year old who can't control his tears and an eleven year old who would rather chop off his toes than be seen crying.)

I must admit that half the time spent at *Dads & Lads* seems to be used up dealing with tears (you get a football in your face and you know about it), disputed goals (when the post is a soft fleecy pullover, can a ball go in-off?) and internecine struggles about who is playing where. One minute, all of them are refusing to go in goal; the next, unfathomably, they all want to be the goalkeeper; then, when awarded the position after long negotiation, they want to come out two minutes later. As a Dad, you know that *Other Things Are Going On*, but you can't figure out what.

Of course, with all the other dads present, you have to exhibit the patience of Job and the wisdom of the Buddha, when you really just want to growl and cuff them round the ear.

The boys make too much of a ball in the face (what's wrong with a bloody nose now and again? Kids these days!), a knock taken in a tackle (come on, a broken ankle never hurt anyone!) or bad weather (hailstones and freezing fog are good for your lungs, sonny. You have to be an all-weather player, you know!). In fact, they're getting a bit fed up with my regular mantra of *Walk it off, that's what the professional players do.* That's right – bloody nose, twisted ankle, frostbite – I tell them to *walk it off*. If one of them had a leg amputated, I'd probably tell him to walk it off.

Then the other day one of the lads belted the ball hard and from a short distance straight into my wedding equipment. I sank to my knees with a groan only to be surrounded by half a dozen gleeful little orcs singing, *Walk it off! Walk it off!*, right in my face.

When I was a boy, I loved playing adults at football; it made the game real. Any kickabout involving dads elevated the status of the game. My family used to take regular summer holidays in Rhyl, North Wales, at a place called the Coventry Co-op Camp (like the Derbyshire miners' holiday camp but without the glitz and glamour). Accommodation was in very basic wooden chalets arranged around a green, and the green was the focus of organised sports: races, cricket, football, rounders.

There was a chalkboard announcing each day's activities. One day, it read: *The Dads challenge the Lads at 2 p.m. because the Lads are RUBBISH!*

The Dads managed to scrape up about nine players, including my old man. At two o'clock, about fifty boys between the ages of four and fourteen turned up. It was decided not to rule anyone out of the fun. The Dads asked if they could have a couple of our players to even up the numbers and we said no; then we conceded and gave them a couple of four year olds. The Lads flung themselves at the Dads, who for the next hour had little kids hanging from their belts, from their shirts and from the seat of their pants. The Lads won 27–0 and it was very satisfying to write this on the chalkboard. To this day, my dad maintains that the Dads let us win.

I don't know about that, but over in Leicester's Knighton Park of a Sunday morning we do generally let the Lads win, though it's important that we sometimes let them lose, too. Both things have to happen. When our boys lost against us for the very first time, one or two of them did get a bit John Terry about it and there were real tears, but they have to learn how to get over it quickly, how to deal with defeat and find a desire to come back stronger. You wouldn't want them to grow up like the captain of our national team.

There is a tree near the spot where we put coats down to make the goalposts. It's called the Sulky Tree. When one of the lads is having a moment, he will always go behind the tree to hide his face. He will always come back after a while. As they get older, the Lads are making less use of the tree. Football leaves boys completely exposed. As an adult, you just get better at hiding the same stuff behind your face.

Anyway, the football is developing fast. It's dawning on some of them that passing is the way to score goals, that arguing about silly things wastes time, that you need to keep your eyes open when trying to head the ball and that you can't take the ball home if the game isn't going your way. This is the Dads I'm talking about.

The old goalkeeping question keeps rearing its head. Some of the boys just don't ever want to do it. (My boy likes playing in goal – but only sometimes – and my heart squeezes to see him in his little goalie shirt and gloves.) Those who do play in goal can't seem to deal with the exposure and the emotional roller-coaster that comes with the position. Kids wear their hearts on their sleeves. If they make a couple of saves, they are lions. If they fumble one in, they come over pale and disaffected, and look for someone else to take a turn.

I know, boys, I know. Being a goalie makes you cry. And worse.

'*You must be barmy.*'

Those words from my dad did come back to haunt me when I was 16. I was playing for my school team – Nicholas Chamberlaine comprehensive in Bedworth – in a cup game on a mild Saturday afternoon when I ended up in Accident and Emergency after taking a boot in the face. The events between getting kicked in the head and the moment before receiving treatment – about an hour – are permanently erased from my memory, even though, by all accounts, I was on my feet and talking.

The team were doing well – Nicholas Chamberlaine had a good pool of players to draw on – when an opposing striker bustled his way into the penalty area, leaving my defenders for dead. It was a one-on-one. As a goalie, you have to go out to meet him. I was already advancing when he poked the ball too far ahead of him, and I knew it was mine. I sprinted out and went down to gather it. I even had time to see the oncoming striker draw back his foot *after* I'd gathered the ball.

Then the lights went out.

Most strikers – even at the highest competitive level – know the dangers involved in kicking – with reinforced football boots – the goalkeeper in the head. Even in the case of a genuine 50–50, most strikers, recognising that this is not warfare after all but a game played for recreation and enjoyment, will, even if their momentum is carrying them forward, leap the goalkeeper as he gathers the ball. It's called sportsmanship. This notion depends on human decency and self-control, and I'm glad to say that most human beings are in reasonable possession of these qualities.

Sadly, not everyone. To follow through on a 50–50 or less in such a situation is a cardinal sin and changes the terms of the game from aggressive competition to violent conflict. Only the real shits do it.

Even though I'd gathered the ball well ahead of him, the murderous schoolboy shit followed through. The hardened toe of his boot thudded against my forehead and his stud lifted off my eyebrow and the skin beneath it. I was out cold.

The next thing I knew I was sitting in the Accident and Emergency ward of the George Eliot hospital in Nuneaton, trying to stop blood running into my eye. My head was pounding. I was still wearing my kit and boots, and all the green in my goalie's sweater was soaked in black-red blood. Part congealed, it was still sticky. I was wearing someone's coat – a man's houndstooth sports jacket a size or two too large. I touched the wound and the blood started flowing into my eye again. Several nurses walked by, clearly too busy with other matters to attend to me. For ten minutes, I sat on a plastic chair trying to stop the blood dripping onto the jacket that someone had kindly draped round my shoulders.

Finally, an Indian doctor walked by, did a double take on me and spoke sharply to one of the nurses. She looked irritated but came over and put some tape over my eye. I didn't know at the time that hospital staff are generally unsympathetic to football injuries, tending to regard them as self-induced. I don't blame them for this: they're overworked just dealing with genuine accidents. No one forces you to play football.

A few minutes later, a man I'd never seen before in my life showed up with tea in a plastic cup. 'Do you take sugar?'

'Uh, three.' (The sugar: I was working class in those days.) 'Is this your coat?' I asked.

He looked at me oddly, then stirred the sugar into the tea. 'Yes.' He looked very concerned. 'Do you know where you just came from?'

'Football. You'd better have the coat back. I'll get blood on it.'

'Keep it on. You should stay warm. I don't care about the jacket.'

I wanted to ask him who he was, but I thought it sounded rude. Finally, I got to see a doctor and my wound was stitched up. There was some discussion about whether I could go home. The doctor kept holding fingers up in front of my face until finally he decided that I could. The owner of the jacket was still patiently awaiting me, and he drove me home. My mother answered the door and turned pale. The man explained that he was the father of one of the lads in the opposing team, though not of the boy who had kicked me unconscious. My mum invited the stranger in and gave him another cup of tea. Two sugars for him.

My dad came in and had a look at the stitches. 'I've told him about this,' he said to the man. The way they talked to each other I might not have been present in the room. He and the stranger joked a lot about my having a black eye in the morning.

They were right about that; in fact, I had two. The heavy bruising fully encircled both eyes and joined in the middle. For three weeks, I looked like the fucking Lone Ranger.

But it's in the job. There's the ball, go out and get it. Or be a crocus.

The smash in the face from the centre-forward's boot happens to a lot of goalies. I saw Ian Wright, a player I loved to watch, unnecessarily follow through on Coventry's goalkeeper, Steve Ogrizovic. Oggy was carried off on a stretcher and, never the best looking of soccer stars to begin with, had a nose like a pirate's hook for the rest of his career. (Ogrizovic was later the subject of a bizarre Internet campaign to get him released from imprisonment on spying charges in Kazakhstan. I was going to sign the petition and maybe send a fiver before I found out that Kazakhstan was well known for its hospitality to bent-nosed former Coventry City goalkeepers. Yes, it was a hoax. It was a country he'd never been to in his life.)

Then there was the horrific head injury to Chelsea's superb Peter Cech. A minute into a game against Reading, Cech's head collided with Stephen Hunt's knee, leaving him concussed. He was rushed to hospital and that evening underwent surgery for a depressed fracture of the skull. The incident split football pundits – although because so many pundits are moral idiots many appeared to back Hunt's right to go for the challenge. Football is often shocking and stupid.

Slow replays clearly showed that Cech had the ball firmly in his grasp before Hunt's knee smashed his skull. He may not have intended to injure the goalkeeper, but he certainly left a marker, a professional calling card that lets another player know he's up against a hard case. Everyone in football knows this happens. Yet what's to debate? Look at the rules of the game: a challenge that endangers safety is serious foul play, earning a compulsory sending off with a three-match ban. In 50–50 ball situations, unless the keeper is going for the same ball with his feet, an attacking player has to back out, otherwise he is endangering safety. And don't make the prissy claim that the goalkeeper is endangering his own safety because everyone is doing that just by playing football. That's why hospital nurses aren't in a hurry to fix your wounds.

If the oncoming striker has made a first touch before the keeper dives, that's different. But if it's a race for the ball and the keeper has collected, then it is the striker's responsibility to draw back or jump over the man on the floor.

Even if the result was an accident it was still a foul, and Hunt should have been sent off. If not, we're into the Last Days of Rome football and might as well play with weapons drawn.

Arm the keeper with spiked gloves, I say. How do you like that idea?

Football is such a serious business, at every level. Look at how some excellent women's football is 'tolerated'. See what happens when a female wants to join in an all-male game. If it is allowed – and it's usually resented by all boys and many men – the tension goes out of the game. It changes gear. That's because it's not really permitted to play football for sport alone; in fact, the difficult truth of it is that the sport is encased in the hostility and aggression of football.

The only time I ever saw this work to the contrary was when I was about ten years old and my family had a visit from my aunt Evelyn from up north. In fact, I should write that it was my great-aunt Evelyn – my dad's aunt, sister to his mother who had died when he was about seven. They lived in Spennymoor. Evelyn, a burly and somewhat brawny woman, had taken him and raised him, and she was kindness itself. She and my pipe-smoking uncle Jim had a number of relatives in Coventry and occasionally they made the trip to the Midlands and did the rounds. We'd have to give up our beds for them and sleep on the floor when they stayed for a couple of nights.

One time when Evelyn and Jim were visiting, my mum and dad had taken Jim off somewhere, leaving Evelyn in charge to 'mind the bairns', as she used to say. Some boys came to the door, wanting to know if I was playing football. Behind our back garden, between the houses, there was a scrap of wasteland. The kids would assemble there for games of all kinds, and just like everyone else we would throw down coats or jumpers on the ground as makeshift goalposts.

'Wor Jackie Milburn!' Evelyn said to me, her eyes flashing. 'Gang, bonnie lad! Get yer ganzies and yer byuts and gang oot with the lads and play fyutbahal!' Mass media has all but smoothed away the gorgeous wrinkles of local dialect, more's the pity.

Back then I didn't understand the biggest half of what she said to me, but, anyway, I got the message. A boy doesn't need to speak a County Durham version of Viking English to know when he's been given permission to go out.

We got out onto the apron of wasteland and tried to pick sides. There was a lot of moaning on that particular day. There were nine lads, which meant four would play five. I was on the side of four and no one wanted to play goalkeeper, me included. (This was before I'd heard the call.) The wrangling and moaning and trading of useless little kids amongst the nine seemed endless. Then Evelyn, who'd come out to take a look at us, popped her head over the garden fence. She had plastic curlers in her hair.

'Are you clartin? Eeee, whativers wrang wi' yez? Yer all like a drip that nivir dropt, man.'

'We haven't got a goalkeeper,' I protested lamely.

'Well, but why don't *you* gang in the net, wor Graham?'

'Eh? No.'

'Wait a minute,' she said. 'Eeee, but I'll not stay long 'cause I'm to cook the dinner.'

She disappeared and then, to my dismay, reappeared

wearing some old gardening boots of my mother's, still bearing her pinafore. She rolled up her sleeves to reveal that brawny pair of arms. The other boys looked at me in horror and revulsion, as if I had the power to stop this. I knew that they were also processing private thoughts about the nature of my family gene pool.

'I'm in the net. Away, lads, away. Eeee! Who's on my side?' She took up position in one of the goals, arms akimbo, fists dug into her hips.

The boys were looking to me to make some sort of protest, but it was beyond me to do so. Great-aunt Evelyn had somehow asserted herself over the game and installed herself in goal.

So we played. Evelyn simply employed the technique of interposing her considerable bulk between the ball and the goal to stop the other team from scoring. She loved every minute of it. She exulted. I remember her eyes flashing every time the ball came near her and her shouting something about how she was good enough to play for Bishop Auckland, which at the time I thought was something to do with the Church. If the ball came along the grass, she swept it away with a stiff leg. If it came at her above waist height, she lifted both fists like a pugilist and punched the ball into touch. Unorthodox goalkeeping, to say the least. The boys on the other team did their damnedest to score past her; the stakes for football on that scrap of wasteland had never seemed quite so high.

If it's possible to admit it, I was appalled and impressed at the same time. It seems sort of magnificent now, but at the time, for a ten year old to be associated with this large woman in plastic curlers, it seemed somewhat disastrous.

'Eeee, I'm clammin!' she said, giving another high ball a right hook before wiping perspiration from her neck. After about half an hour, without having conceded a goal, she waddled away, muttering darkly about shelling some peas. We boys carried on playing for a while longer, but the truth was that a contagious energy and something else rather special had walked out of the game with her.

My great-aunt Evelyn and René Higuita would have got along famously. They could have smoked Cuban cigars and talked about how goalkeeping is about having fun.

'What is the point of it all,' says René, puff, puff, puff on his cigar, hand-rolled on a virgin's thigh, etc., 'if you can't have fun?'

'Eee! Yer not far wrong, wor René!' Puff, puff. 'These cigars are canny good. Whees i' the netty?'

'What?'

And so on. I want to have fun when I play in goal. And sometimes I do. But against the Hungarians, it's not working out. I make a poor clearance from a back pass and it drops to one of their players on the halfway line. He makes a simple, incisive pass through the channel, and one of their forwards locks onto it and slots it past me.

That's two crappy goals, and I feel responsible for both of them. Of course it would help if my team got a single shot on goal, but in the entire 90 minutes we don't seem to be able to manage that. So, I'm left to replay my errors over and over on the back of my retina and think how the world could have been a better place.

Maybe I should write a poem about how each of these goals came about. Mention Braille. Get them published.

Nah.

I must have made a couple of saves during the Hungary game because I was left nursing two sprained fingers on my left hand and one on my right. That's another thing about being a goalie: Fat Finger Syndrome. I don't smoke any more, but with sausage fingers you could never hold a cigarette properly for your post-match smoke. Jake Wallis Simons is deputy goalkeeper in case I have to be substituted. But he recently put himself out of action. He was cutting his toenails with a Swiss army knife (this is true) and stabbed his big toe. There you are: another safe pair of hands.

So, that's it then. We lose our second game to the Magyars and sit in the dressing-room discussing who's going to be first to try a swig of the Hungarian glak.

The final of the Writers' World Cup is between Italy and Sweden. Funny that. You wouldn't expect the two teams who progress to the final to be the ones fielding the highest number of semi-pros, full pros and capped internationals, would you? You wouldn't expect it to be the two teams with the most flexible interpretation of the rules of who can be nominated as a writer, would you? Funny that.

All things considered, we watch the final from the stands with good grace. It goes to penalties. And guess what? Swedish international goalkeeper Tommy Olofsson (all right, Sweden Writers' XI goalkeeper) knows all about the penalty hall of mirrors. He does that thing I mentioned earlier of standing at the side of the goal while the Italian spot-kickers place their ball. Olofsson seems to mesmerise them by coolly puffing on his pipe between penalties. Yes, you thought I was joking! He's not to be rushed! He even deliberately lights up his pipe all over again for a few puffs while the Italians wait to take their kick.

Now, Olofsson is no fool. He's made a study of James Joyce – the poet of the unconscious mind, pretty much unfathomable in any language. What Olofsson knows is that while the spot-kicker can repress his telltales and giveaway signs while facing the keeper, he won't while he thinks no one is watching. When he's ready, he docks his pipe on the goalpost, hitches up his baggy goalie's pants and takes up position. The first Italian penalty taker blasts the ball straight at him. So does the next. And then the next blasts wide. The Swedes just need to put the third penalty away.

They do so.

They'll be insufferable in the bar.

So, the Writers' World Cup tournament is all over. England Writers' XI emerge from the competition with the wooden spoon. But we've learned some important things. I can't for the life of me think what they are, but that's what you say at these times. I seem to have spent my whole life hearing government departments, social services, health trusts, social work agencies and the judicial system apologising for some failure or other but assuring the public that this will be a learning experience. So, why can't we do the same?

This has been a learning experience. We're prepared to learn from our mistakes. The important thing is to make sure that this never happens again.

The only thing left to do is enjoy an evening partying with the other players on our last evening in Florence. The Swedes are in an exuberant mood after their victory. Well, that's an understatement; in fact, their mood is almost psychotic. They sing loudly in a vexatious fashion, banging their glasses on the table as they do so. They look like Vikings, slamming their tankards in the mead hall. In praise of Odin! They taunt us with the name of 'Sven-Göran Eriksson la la la la la' to the tune of 'Brown Girl in the Ring'. Then they start singing 'Brown Girl in the Ring', oblivious or insensitive to the presence of Patrick Neate's beautiful Zimbabwean wife, who happens to be the only girl in the ring who is . . . oh, I don't know. But it's not sour grapes when I say that the Swedish celebrations have a drunken and slightly nightmarish quality.

But then they suddenly stop singing and announce, slurring and smiling, that they are hosting another such tournament next year in Malmö, and all expenses will be found. The Italian team look at the English team, and the English team look at the Hungarian team, and the Hungarian team look at the Italian team, and we all think: someone on the Swedish team is going to have a huge financial hangover in the morning. We're going to get to do this all over again! We thank the Swedes for this wonderful promise and invite them to sing some more Viking songs.

The England team award 'player of the tournament' trophies to Haydn Middleton and me. It's an old farts award really – *Christ, these old boys are still breathing!* – since we're both in our 50s. Though, in Haydn's case, he really is our man of the tournament.

'We're doing it again. Next year. In Sweden.'

'Who's paying for it?'

'Sponsorship, Dad. Someone sponsors it all.'

'Who?'

'I dunno, Dad.'

'Is it for charity?'

'No, I told you that before, Dad.'

'So, they're going to sponsor you again? *You?*'

'Well, there's not just me. There's Andrew Smith and Craig Taylor . . .' And we go through it all again.

'You must be bloody barmy.'

It's not that our England Writers' team in Italy was awful. Well, it was, but it was just that we didn't get enough opportunities to practise together as a unit. So Phil gets to work on that, trying to line up a few fixtures before Malmö and our return to the World Cup stage. Titter. But it's not easy. There just aren't that many teams of mostly past-it blokes who only play four times a year. Most teams, of course, play rugged football on a weekly basis. The players are all mostly under 35, and if they're not then they are usually dedicated fitness fanatics. We need to find footballers like us. Hopeless fantasists. Deluded deadbeats.

We do get a few fixtures sorted. We play a Comedians' XI – yes, ha, ha, ha, and all that – down at Crystal Palace sports centre. They are a mixture of stand-ups and actors

I recognise from TV adverts. We seem to spend a lot of time saying, 'Wasn't he in that advert for Jewsons?' and 'No, you're thinking of Pizza Shed.' I think they have a unicyclist in their squad, too. Sadly, they don't play in red noses, nor do they make annoying cracks to put you off your shot or anything like that. On a skill level, they are about on a par with us, and the fact that they go down to ten men allows us to get the better of them, as we run out 4–2 winners.

There are a couple of other fixtures: we lose narrowly to Manchester Divorced Dads and then get walloped in Stepney by Sporting Bengali, who kindly take their foot off the gas after going 4–0 up ridiculously early. This team actually drew with the Indian national soccer team, so we don't have to feel too bad about it. If we don't want to.

These games are also a chance to recruit a couple of new players – or at least try to. Paul Laity, a journalist from *The Guardian*, comes into the defence and is no slouch, and neither is top-bloke Jakob von Baeyer. Will Skidelsky, books editor for *The Observer*, has a very useful foot. Another reviewer whom I don't recognise also lines up for us against Sporting Bengali; he runs around for ten minutes before staggering towards me, breathless, clutching his ribs like he's been run through with a sword. He leans against my goalpost looking distinctly faint then promptly vomits inside the net. 'Fuck this,' he says. He heads back to the changing-room and I never see him again. I must remember to find out who he was.

In the rainy season that is the grey days between glamorous writers' football tournaments, I try to keep my eye in by playing six-a-side. I seriously doubt whether it's helpful to a goalkeeper. The tiny goals seem almost too easy to protect and they mess with your sense of the angle, causing you to advance further off your line than maybe you would for a full-size goal. But I want to recover some of my lost skills, if I can.

I believe in the mythology that the skills were there once upon a time and that they've been lost. You know, the self-deception of a Golden Age. Atlantis. Someone in the family who once had money.

Then before we know it, it's Malmö in the sunshine: a brand-new World Cup tournament and a chance to improve our lowly ranking. Hello again to the Hungarians and the Italians and the Swedes. What's more, the tournament has been swelled by the presence of the Danes and the Germans. The Writers' World Cup is expanding. There's excited talk about an American team joining in the fray next year, and an Israeli Writers' XI, and an Iraqi team too. I don't know how that's going to shape up, or who the hell is poised to pour more money into this unlikely scenario, but anyway the prospects for the tournament just get better all the time. Or more ridiculous, depending on your point of view.

But in Malmö, meanwhile, there's something amiss with the draw. Sweden, the hosts, face Denmark one day and Germany the next. We, the English, because of our exceptional stamina and youth, and because of the skills we demonstrated in Florence, get to play Italy in the morning of the first day and Hungary in the afternoon. The second game starts 90 minutes after the conclusion of the first. Surely, some mistake?

'What are we going to do with all that time between the two games?' Haydn Middleton wants to know.

Challenged, our warm, generous and charming Swedish hosts explain that this timetable was arranged 'to cause less difficulty with travel arrangements'. Uh? Right. Well, when we're all such good mates off the field it's not like we're going to lodge a protest with Sepp Blatter at Fifa, is it? Plus Swedish hospitality is so damn good that it would be churlish to complain too loudly.

We've recruited a couple of new faces and lost some old ones who couldn't make the tournament. Wearing the three lions this time will be Dave Goldie, a Scottish academic and essayist. It's a wonderful thing to watch a Scotsman in this situation. There's a mixture of honest pride and clannish repugnance at war in his handsome face as he pulls on the England shirt. The phrase 'cognitive dissonance' seems apt because these diametrically opposed sentiments have set up a kind of vibration inside his skull. Another new recruit to the line is Simon Kuper, author of the classic examination of politics in the game, *Football Against the Enemy*.

And so we face the Italians – again – with their silky skills and their semi-pros and their former Serie A stars. But this time we're tighter, much better organised and it shows. In the second half, disaster strikes as our veteran midfield general Haydn Middleton has to go off with a serious calf injury, but Dave Goldie, in particular, is an inspiration, holding the back line together. It's a measure of our improvement that with three minutes to go we are holding the Italians to a 2–2 scoreline.

I'm bellowing at my teammates just to keep it very tight in the middle and to hold shape at the back; we'll settle for 2–2. But do they listen to their goalkeeper? No. A couple of the useless, over-educated, undisciplined idiots in my godforsaken team go for a feeble through-play and get dispossessed inside the centre circle. We're left in a ragged state and they easily slot a ball through the middle, which is picked up by my old mate Francesco Trento, the switchblade of the Italian attack, always threatening on the left wing. He bursts through on his own.

Now, I've so far managed to shut Francesco out here in Sweden, just as I did in Italy. I've got lucky on both occasions and I know it. But he doesn't know that. I jinxed him in Florence, and he's starting to wonder if he'll ever slot one past me. Now he's clean through and we've both got *too much time* to think.

For a goalkeeper in a one-on-one situation, there is no question: you have to come out. You have to come off your line. It's imperative. But there's an optimum position for the advance. The angle for the attacker reduces, as you come out: everyone knows that. But what everyone doesn't grasp is that if you advance beyond a certain position (I have in my head an imaginary semicircle drawn from the goalposts and passing midway between the six-yard line and the penalty spot), then all an attacking player has to do is step left or right with the ball and the goal angle opens up again proportionately. Plus there is always the option of chipping the ball over the goalkeeper's head.

I've got too much time, and I think I want to bully Francesco into making the chip. During the two games, he's broken through several times now on these one-on-ones and every time I've saved or forced him to shoot wide. Because I know he's frustrated, I'm sure I can force him into the chip. And there is an answer to the chipped shot.

If you are sure there's a chip coming, you get as close as you can to the attacker, leap high with arms extended forward and crash down the chip. A chip, by its very nature, is a slow shot, and a goalie has a reasonable chance of success with this attempted stop. I've done it a couple of times. There's risk, of course: if you leap too early, the striker could simply roll the ball under you and you're left looking like a lemon. But you'll see the chip coming before it's executed, and if you're out there fast enough you have a good chance.

Francesco sees me coming and he flips the ball up for the chip. My plan is working, all right. Except that his chip is perfectly measured: high, strong and accurate. It slots into the net behind me: 3–2.

Why didn't I just let him come at me and shoot, when my record against him had been so good? Why the hell did I think I could do that . . . when I was winning already? *What kind of a goalkeeper is the one who is not tormented by the goal he has allowed?* asked Lev Yashin. *He must be tormented! And if he is calm, that means the end.*

Too much time. Too much brains. Not enough sense. What's-his-name . . . Bronowski's balls-up. My advice to young goalkeepers: don't have anything to do with it.

We're beaten by the Italians again.

Gelati.

I like to make up for my lack of goalkeeping skills by having a big mouth. It pays for a goalkeeper to have a big mouth. I like to encourage my back line by alerting them to dangers and barking instructions, like I know what I'm talking about. Of course I don't know what I'm talking about, but I make out like I do. You can even fool the opposition – a bit – if you have a big mouth.

The first thing a goalie has to learn to shout is, 'Keeper!' That means, 'I'm getting that ball and if you get in my way you'll get clobbered, and don't come crying to me about it, you big stupid baby.' Or something like that. Anyway, it's designed to keep your own defenders out of the way; but as a young keeper, I noticed an extraordinary thing, and that was this: if you bellow loud enough and hard enough, it sometimes seems to persuade the opposing strikers that they have no chance of getting that ball, so they back off. It doesn't always work, and it's partly psychological, but if you sound like you're either going to grab the ball or twist someone's head off in doing so, they do tend to inch back a bit.

It's bizarre. I'm sure that at professional level players are trained to resist this. After all, what you're doing is *talking* people out of going for the ball. But at sub-pro level, it often works.

It's vital to be able to communicate with your team, but it's also part of establishing the presence I mentioned earlier. There are only a few under-pressure words that I can think of that a keeper needs. *Away!* is a clear command for a clearance; *Back!* is a command for a back pass; *Press!* is there if one of your teammates is standing off an opponent. There are some other words you say when you let a goal in, but these are the essential bellowed instructions. As a writer who spends his days modelling with words, I love it that I can be in a situation where I can get life – well, 90 minutes of footballing life – down to three verbs and a noun. I'm working on trimming it down still further, to *Ug!* and *Ack!* Anyway, I like shouting. I like feeling primitive.

Some defenders have a habit of shouting *Keeper's!*, if they think the ball has your name on it. This can be both helpful and unhelpful. You and you alone need to decide if it's the keeper's ball; sometimes a defender will shout *Keeper's!* and thereby give himself permission to give up his chase or interest in the ball. If he makes a bad call, he can put you in a very sticky situation. The very fact that he has called *Keeper's!* can make it look like you should have got to the ball, when really it was his job to stay with the chase. In this way, sometimes your own defender can make you look bloody stupid. If this happens, then you have to turn your ugly big mouth on your own defender in such a way that he will be discouraged from ever doing that again. Really, you have to burn his hair off if he pulls that one on you.

There are other instructions to be offered because, once again, goalkeepers do have a different or advantaged position. Our vision of the game is a unique one. Our field of vision is wider. A defender watching the ball midfield might not see a winger making a run beyond his left shoulder; he might miss an overlapping player arriving; he might be unaware that he's playing an attacker onside. There are many possibilities and it is the goalie's job to keep his defenders awake to all dangers and possibilities.

The keeper can also help the back line to keep its shape. If the line spreads too wide, the ball through the channel is a perpetual menace; too bunched, and the wide danger is obviously exposed. A goalie can also try to stop his players from diving in when what they really need to do is stay goal-side and on their feet.

Finally, you can use your vocal cords to marshal the defenders in front of you, trying to ensure that no shots come in at you without pressure on the striker.

It's outrageous really. I play behind players who are much better footballers than I am, roaring at them as if I know more about the game than they do, as if I'm somehow superior, more experienced, more insightful; as if I have some God-given right to speak to them in this way.

Well, I do. I'm the goalie. I'm the dog at the gate, and I bark myself hoarse.

I've been yellow-carded only twice in my entire football career, and I've never been sent off. The first time I was booked was as a college player.

One of my defenders was injured in a crunching tackle: he lay sprawled in the six-yard box, while the ball bobbled about in the penalty area. The ball wouldn't go out of play and the opposition showed no sign of playing the ball into touch. This sporting gesture just wasn't the norm at the time. If you were badly injured, you were just expected to lie down and either die or groan theatrically until the ball went out of play naturally.

But I could see my teammate was in a bad way. He wasn't moving an inch, which is always a sign that something might be seriously wrong. Plus his face was very pale. A shot came in at me and I saved it. I got up, did the old-fashioned bounce-bounce routine and booted it out of touch beyond the halfway line, so that my pal could get some attention. The referee booked me, as we used to call it back then, the equivalent of a yellow card: unsporting behaviour. As it happened, my defender had a broken ankle, but that didn't change anything.

There was another small problem. When the ref trotted over to me with his little black book at the ready, the captain of our college team came up to me and said, 'Don't argue about it, *Chris*.'

Chris? I thought.

'I'm not arguing,' I replied.

'Look, *Chris*,' he said again, 'don't argue with the ref. It's not worth it, *Chris*.'

'He's not arguing,' said the ref, on my behalf.

'*Chris* does argue,' my captain said. 'I've told him not to.'

What the fuck is the matter with him? I thought. Then the referee asked me for my name and I saw my captain's eyebrow was winched pretty high. It dawned on me that I'd failed to register my name with the local football association, since I only tended to play whenever they needed cover; the team could get into big trouble with the junta who ran the local leagues at the time, and who were known to impose fines on clubs even if they were reported for having mismatching socks.

'Name,' said the ref.

'Chris Heald,' I said, giving him the name of the regular keeper.

Chris, in the unlikely event you ever read this, I got you booked. Soz.

So, the only time I really, really got yellow-carded was in Malmö, versus Hungary. Less than two hours after the game against Italy, we were expected to line up against the Magyars. Well, it was a pretty tall order for a bunch of pen-pushers. We had nothing left in the reserve tank.

As for me, my left calf had gone completely dead from a knock I'd taken in the Italy game. Seized, I think is the word. We'd been assigned a physiotherapist – a shy and retiring, bespectacled Swede – but Dave Goldie had scared him away. After the first match, someone had asked him if he had any ice, and when he asked what the ice was for he was told it was for putting in the vodka and tonic. He got the joke late and offered a polite laugh, rubbing his chin nervously. So, when Dave Goldie, who genuinely had a slight groin strain, approached him with his hand inside his shorts, jiggling his wedding tackle, the Swedish physio looked alarmed. Goldie asked if a 'wee rub' might be possible in the injured region, closing in and advertising his problem with yet another jiggle. The physio ran out of the changing-room.

'Was it something I said?' Goldie wanted to know.

No one saw our assigned physio for the rest of the tournament. And what with everyone cramping and seizing up, we could have done with his services. We were wooden lumps against Hungary.

It was like the first game against Italy all over again. The killer through-ball was slashing us apart, and the useless bastards in front of me just wouldn't keep their shape. The Hungarians were given far too many strike opportunities. I stopped a few shots, let a couple in. Very tired, we were 2–0 down with ten minutes to go. The Hungarian central striker broke free as far back as the halfway line and no one in my team had the legs to even give him a chase. I ran well off my line and made my best save of the tournament, going full length to my left to keep him out. Thing is, I'd travelled three yards or more outside my penalty box to make the stop, and the Hungarians wanted me sent off.

To be sure, it's a sending-off offence, no question of that. There were six or seven Hungarian red shirts surrounding the Swedish referee, hotly demanding that I walk. It seemed to me a bit unnecessary. The Hungarians were all over us and we clearly had no way back. Half of our team were limping. But the rules say I should have been sent off, and the Hungarian impalers wanted blood – my blood.

You can stand there and look guilty and help the ref to make the decision to send you off, or you can walk back to your goal, take up position, rub your hands together and assume a posture that suggests it's going to require an earth-mover to get you to budge (or that you're so dumb you don't realise what you've done). Well, it might work sometimes. The Swedish ref was no fool. He waved the Hungarian blood-guzzlers away and ran over to me. 'I should send you off, but I'm in a good mood today.' He waved the yellow, not the red.

The next day we'd recovered enough to give Denmark a proper game. The Danish writers were a thoroughly likeable mob who'd spent the previous night drinking and clubbing. A closely fought game went 2–0 in our favour. They rattled the crossbar from a thunderous free-kick, but I'd managed to get my wall lined up before the kick was taken, and I call that progress.

The first England victory!

I love my teammates. I could kiss their big, fat, ugly lips.

'Is your eye OK?'

'Yeah, fine.'

'You sure? Looks a bit sore.'

'No problem at all.'

When you're a lad, you can play football at a second's notice. At my age, the preparation for a match is longer than the game. I have to go through all these complex stretching exercises that feel vaguely fraudulent, but if you don't do them you'll be hobbling off the pitch within the first three minutes. Then there's the matter of strapping on knee supports and ankle supports until underneath your goalie's kit you're trussed up like an Egyptian mummy. Oh, and then there is the contact lens.

I seem to be better at getting to the short stops than the long strikes blasted from outside the penalty area. It doesn't make much sense, since they were always easier to save in my youth, and I can't blame it all on the stunt balls. The main difference between then and now is that my eyesight has faded, probably from writing too many crap novels, but possibly from advanced age. Yeah, that would be it.

I wear spectacles for driving, going to the cinema, watching TV and so on. I wanted to do something about this issue of the balls from outside the penalty area, and you can't wear specs on the pitch. Well, you can: Nick Royle in our team has some of those special sporting goggles. He looks like he should have a snorkel and a pair of big, black rubber flippers to go with them, but they seem to work for him. I just can't imagine being a scuba-diving goalie, so I rejected that option.

There is, then, the sporting contact lens.

I've no interest in wearing contact lenses for reasons of vanity. In fact, wearing ordinary spectacles, according to my wife, makes me look less of a thug. But contact lenses . . . my God, you have to be utterly dedicated.

'Have you got it in yet?' My wife. I was 'practising' with my new soft lens. I didn't want to be in a position where I turned up for a game and wasn't familiar with putting the thing in. So far it had been about three hours. We were supposed to be going to a party.

So, in addition to all the exercises and the swathes of muscular support, there is now the ritual of the contact lens. I'm 'lucky' in that I only have to use one lens. (Apparently, the other eye is completely useless.) Yet I get through my supply of lenses at the rate of about one every fifteen minutes. They split after too much handling. I feel like it's in, then it's not, and it's hanging on my tear-soaked cheek.

Finally, it goes in. I'm ready.

'Jesus, that looks sore!'

I always wanted to look like Gordon Banks. So, I made it. The one-eyed goalkeeper. I check it out in the mirror. After being poked and stroked and thumbed and pressed and squeezed for a couple of hours, my single, swollen, livid red eye reminds me of the figure of Cyclops from Greek mythology.

'Is your eye OK?' It's what my fellow players say to me in the dressing-room. All of them. 'Christ, that looks sore.'

There is only one thing worse than inserting a contact lens. It's getting it out afterwards.

Goalkeeping is exactly like writing, in that you always get some idiot mouthing clichés like: 'Good goalkeepers are born, not made.' There is always this or that pompous, stuck-up prig of a writer who thinks that writers are members of a kind of priesthood, who say that writing can't be taught. What this means is they are lousy teachers who can't even impart the skill of sharpening a pencil.

Goalkeepers can and need to be trained; there's just so little of it outside the serious 'soccer academy' level. All my schoolboy training was on the job, during games. My position would have been strengthened enormously if someone had spent some time lobbing balls for me, to improve my catching technique, or my footwork, or my recovery speed. I'm just making the point that any schoolboy goalie could quickly be advanced from being a decent keeper to a good one.

I spent too many of my primary and later school games allowing my burly centre-half to take the goalkicks because of his superior range. When I came to have trials for the county schoolboy team, the selector chose the keeper on the strength of his goalkick, nothing else. There were seven or eight goalkeepers called. I got five minutes, in a game where I didn't touch the ball. After the game, the selector asked me to take a goalkick. I did so and it was a bit feeble. So, there you are: after that rigorous examination, my budding professional career was done for.

Following that fiasco, I took a couple of balls up to the football field to practise kicking. Luckily, I had two younger brothers, Martin and David. I lied to them and said I was going to take them for a game, whereas I simply made them fetch the ball back for me – 50 times or more. They were bored out of their skulls and over the last 40 years have never trusted me an inch.

I am fully aware of the complete package that goes to make the perfect keeper. It helps me to analyse my own strengths and weaknesses as a custodian. But I'm wondering if my theory stands up. If you've been paying attention, the theory suggests that a writer's skills are reflected in the way he or she performs on the football pitch. My personal goalkeeping assessment chart runs something like this:

Shot-stopper: Well, not so good since my eyesight started to fade. The ball these days tends to manifest late, as a dark bird swooping out of a torn sky – something that makes you shiver and is to be swatted.

Ability in the air: Er, none. Never been up to much there, truth be told. Always had one eye weaker than the other, so tend to be a bit of a fumbler. Shame that.

Quick reflexes: Ha!

The capacity to read the game in anticipation: Ah, yes, I can do that. But it would be better if I could do something about it.

Good distribution: 'Fraid not.

Since the introduction of the back-pass law, the ability to act as a sweeper within a defensive system: Not with my knees.

Strong vocal presence: Big mouth, you mean? Yes.

Well, that's about it then: big mouth.

How does this all shape up for the theory? All right, fair cop. Don't go on about it.

Guess who lines up against each other for the final of the World Cup in Malmö? Yes, it's the Swedes and the Italians again. Funny that.

Sadly, we don't get a game against the German team. We watch them on the pitch when they play Sweden. They watch us on the pitch when we play Denmark. Both teams fancy it. Yes, a mouth-watering fixture against the Hun, the traditional enemy. There's no question about it: we love playing against the Germans, and they love playing against us.

Mainly, it goes back to the 1966 World Cup final. (Oh, and a couple of world wars might be locked in the psyche too, but mostly it's that World Cup final.) The controversy of whether the ball crossed the line for the third English goal is only a controversy in Germany, of course. We English *know* that the ball crossed the line. I even published a story on how I personally witnessed the ball crossing the line, because I was there as a boy, listening to the final on a transistor radio. The story was called 'As Seen on Radio'.

We were disappointed we didn't get to play them in Sweden. And they say the same. With the Malmö tournament over, we leave with the hope of a game against the Germans sometime in the future.

So passionate is the interest of these two teams to play one another that it miraculously gets organised within a few months of Malmö.

The game is staged in Germany, and so that's how I find myself in the twilight of Berlin one cold autumn evening being driven from the airport in an open-top military Trabant (the kind of eastern European vehicle you once saw on newsreels, casually employed in the machine-gunning of dissidents as they tried to clamber over the Berlin Wall during the Cold War). Also in the truck are Patrick Neate and Jake Wallis Simons.

We've been issued with army-surplus overcoats to ward off the cold, as our driver, Falko Hennig, waltzes the Trabant through the Berlin traffic, tunelessly serenading us with 'Streets of Berlin' – sung in doleful German, of course. We can't seem to stop giggling. (The previous weekend, I'd been asked to speak about my writing at a pagan festival where they torched a giant wicker man; the contrast between the places where the 'writing game' delivers me could not have been more acute.)

We are variously accommodated by the opposition. Nick and I are billeted with the urbane and hospitable German writer Ralf Bönt in his East Berlin apartment. Bönt is a nuclear physicist-turned-novelist. It doesn't seem fair to have *all* the talents, but there he is. (His promising writing career was interrupted after he was poisoned by mercury from a badly filled tooth. He used scientific method to trace the cause of his illness after doctors couldn't find anything wrong with him. He was eventually vindicated when traces of mercury were found to be poisoning his system.)

On the evening before the game, Bönt is the perfect host in every way one could want. In the morning, though, he changes.

'Good morning, Ralf. Sleep well?' I ask.

'I'm sorry,' he announces, 'I can't be friendly.'

'What?'

'I can't be friendly. I enjoyed your company last night, and I already like you both too much. I'm playing against you at 1200 hours. If I'm friendly with you now, I won't have the right psychology for football.'

'Oh, OK. Fair enough. You're not going to poison our breakfasts, are you?'

'I already thought of that and I decided against.' He's suddenly turned into one of those Teutonic knights, with a sneer and a duelling scar.

'Ha, ha. Don't forget you're driving us to the stadium.'

'Yes, I thought about making you take a taxi, but I didn't feel good about that idea. We'll just have to drive in complete silence.'

'Right.'

So, we did. Ralf was utterly focused on the drive through Berlin. Not a word. He was in the zone.

'Are you looking forward to the game, Graham?' Nick asked me, to break the oppressive silence.

'Yes, I notice they have lots of tall players, Nick, so I'm hoping for lots of high crosses. As you know, Nick, I'm very fond of high crosses. Never feel happier than when a high cross comes my way.'

Nick put his hand over his mouth. I saw Ralf clock what I'd said. His English was easily good enough to understand it all, but not good enough to catch the nuance. He was already telling his teammates to keep the ball low against the English keeper.

I was looking forward to the game. The great thing about football is the momentary escape. I'd had a difficult summer. For one thing, I was worried to death about my little boy, who had been poorly all through the school holidays. Then we'd been burgled while we slept upstairs. Then I tried to get a kitchen fitted, which was a delivery nightmare spread across several months. Then my lovely 'you must be barmy' dad was diagnosed with cancer. On and on this stuff went that summer. But you play football, and for 90 minutes you think of nothing else, nothing but the game. For a writer with too much internal noise, too much neurotic interior gibbering going on in his head, football is cleansing and cathartic.

Although it might just take the lid off things, too.

We make a lively start and hit the post in the opening exchanges. Then the Germans break through twice and easily slam the ball past me into the net. I don't even get a sniff of the ball. Later on I get caught out of position, but someone makes a miraculous clearance off the line to get me out of jail. We go in at half-time 2–1 down. I'm not happy because I've only had two shots to save and I haven't got near either of them. Two shots on target, two goals conceded. That doesn't feel like goalkeeping.

After half-time, our boys go after them like hissing snakes, netting three terrific goals within half an hour. With a comfortable 4–2 lead, we have only 15 minutes to play out when I collect an innocuous ball, walk with it to the edge of the area, bounce it a couple of times and boot it upfield. The referee blows his whistle for an infringement.

'What?' I say to him.

He says something in German. I ask one of the German forwards why the ref has blown his whistle. 'Double bounce,' I'm told.

What? Double bounce? Now, let's get this straight. As a keeper, once you have handled the ball, you are not allowed to put it down and pick it up again until it's been played by a member of the opposing team. You are also not allowed to deliberately parry the ball and then pick it up. I guess if you bounce the ball, technically speaking, you are releasing it and then handling it a second time. I have a habit of bouncing the ball before booting it, a habit that goes back to my schoolboy football days. But so do many professional keepers. I've made a point of researching this issue with referees and there's not a ref in all of England, or many other countries around the entire world, who will interpret a bounce as a release. There is one in Germany.

'Double bounce,' he confirms to me. 'Free-kick.'

I'm baffled, my teammates are confused, and even the opposition players are bewildered by this decision. But free-kick it is. Ralf Bönt tipped me off earlier that the match official is someone who enjoys a drink before, during and after the game, but the ref isn't drunk. He is a fully qualified referee – the fact that he has a purple face and has been some 30 yards off the pace of the game throughout shouldn't come into it. What's more, you don't abuse someone who has given up his Saturday morning just so that a load of middle-aged writers can fulfil their daft fantasies about being footballers. You say thank you for refereeing us, and you get on with the game.

It's a free-kick and you build a wall. Oh, that.

The free-kick is right on the edge of the box. Have we got our wall routine in order? Patrick Neate is going to tell me afterwards that I'm apoplectic (again), trying to form the wall in front of me, as the German marksmen place the ball. It's true that I'm shredding my larynx all over again. Then, while I'm positioning myself, one of the German team trots up and stands right in front of me.

Huh? He can't do that, because he's offside, surely. That's unless one of your teammates has suddenly taken it into his head to stand on the goalpost, as per for a corner. It's as I'm bellowing at my wall that I see his white England shirt out of the corner of my eye. Too late: I've been so focused on setting the wall that I haven't told my own player to get the hell out.

The kick is taken low and hard just inside the wall. The German player unsighting me steps aside at the last second and the ball whistles past my legs: 4–3. The fault is mine, no question. I should have moved my defender out, leaving the German player in front of me in an offside position.

We have about seven minutes to hang onto our lead. I'm still cross and baffled by the referee's fairyland double-bounce infringement, which led to the German goal. I'm also aware that Wolfgang Weber equalised for West Germany in the dying seconds of the 1966 World Cup. A traditional Hun trick. Seven minutes.

The Germans come looking for that equaliser. They have a fine midfielder who looks like Mick Hucknall from Simply Red. He fires in a low shot near the upright. Thankfully, I manage to get down and push it round the post. One save in the whole fucking game. Anyway, we're otherwise containing the Hun pretty well. Mick Hucknall collects the ball in the middle of our half and looks to make a diagonal play across the field. It's none other than our charming host, Ralf Bönt, who makes his run towards the box. Nick Royle, guarding the left flank, sees it ahead of time. Nick is an experienced player, so he simply steps upfield, neatly playing Ralf three or four yards offside. But Mick Hucknall plays the ball to Ralf, who runs inside the box and hits a sweet volley right past me.

It won't do him any good. The referee can't possibly have missed the offside.

Well, he gives the goal: 4–4.

For a moment, I'm dumbfounded. Then I start roaring at the referee. I mean, raging and shouting like a moron, a peasant. I can feel the blood rising and scorching my ears. It all comes out. But really it's not that goal. It's my little boy. It's the dirty junkie skank who burgled us while we slept. It's those fucking useless cheats who were supposed to be delivering our kitchen. Hell, it's probably that groundsman at the Barker Butts stadium in Coventry all those years ago. It's all of it. It's why we play football. And it's not always the case, but sometimes the lid just blows.

The referee just takes it. For the things I bellow at him, I should be sent off. It's in another language, but, hell, he has the sentiments nailed precisely. I practically loosen the wax in his ears. He really should reach for the red card in his top pocket. But he absorbs it all.

'Graham, it's OK,' I hear Goldie say behind me. 'It's OK.'

After the game, I will apologise to the referee. Even though I know the goal was offside, I will apologise because it doesn't matter. As Goldie says, it's OK. But when your blood is up, when you're playing football with all the rage and hostility that forms the energy of your game, you are in the grip of other forces. So to the ref who had given up his time so that we could play out our fantasies about being footballers, I do hereby humbly and sincerely apologise. You see, it wasn't you I was shouting at; it was my dad's cancer. I'd like to stand behind the Sulky Tree, but there isn't one.

The game kicks off again and, after a minute or two, I recapture my proper shape and begin to resemble a human being again. I feel pretty sheepish. After all, what about those evenings in Malmö, when I agreed with Paolo Verri and my other Italian friends that we should be constructing a different kind of footballing mentality? I won't be able to until I can stop football from also being about my life. It's in the mix of a game, heart and soul. How am I going to tell Paolo that the revolution might need stronger men than me?

Meanwhile on the field, it looks like the game is going to end in a fair result, the kind of result that asks questions about the competence of both goalkeepers. But it's OK. The sun is shining and the small matter of my ridiculous bellowing at the ref will be forgotten by everyone almost immediately. A fair result: 4–4. There remain about 30 seconds to play, as I remind myself that football in general, and goalkeeping in particular, is about the joy of the athletic moment. It's about having fun.

The German midfielders are just as tired as our boys. Mick Hucknall collects the ball in the midfield and chips it hopefully into the air towards my goal. But his teammates are too knackered to chase it. I stand on the six-yard line waiting for it to drop comfortably into my arms, from where I will boot the ball upfield and the ref will no doubt blow the final whistle.

4–4. We'll all settle for that.

But as the ball drops towards me, it occurs to me that the flight and trajectory of the ball are exactly the same as for René Higuita when he performed his famous scorpion kick. It's about head height, and on target for the goal. I wonder if I can imitate his bit of madness. It's a simple catch, or I could inject some fun into the last few seconds of the game and replicate the scorpion kick. Of course, if I miss it, with the score at 4–4, the consequences will be pretty disastrous. I'll never be able to look my lovely teammates in the eye. On the other hand, a bit of nonsense might atone for my earlier outburst. I mean just like René Higuita, I like to enjoy myself too. Why shouldn't I?

To hell with it, I think. We only come this way once.

With my eye on the ball, I launch myself forward, arms spread wide, like wings. For a moment, I'm like a superhero, flying through the sky. I bring my heels up high behind me, hopefully well timed to make at least some contact with the ball as it loops over me.

The moment freezes as the ball drops towards me and I'm suspended there in time. So are the horrified expressions on the faces of my teammates, as they see what I'm attempting to do. *It's OK*, I want to reassure them. *It's all right*. It's nothing. Or if it's not nothing, it's exactly why you take on the custodian's job. The drama. The keeper's Technicolor shirt of dreams.

It's just simple goalkeeping made spectacular.

THANKS

To all my dazzling teammates, for whom I've only once kept a clean sheet. Special mention to Phil Oltermann, team organiser, who checked this manuscript for insults to fellow writers and said there should be more. To Sutton and District Referees Society's 'Ask Agatha', for answering questions about the rules concerning goalkeepers. To Debs Warner, for showing a superb pair of editing hands and preventing own goals. And to all the *Dads & Lads*: Neville, James, Steve, George, Eddie, Dave, Samuel, Luke, Mark, Louie, Brendon, Declan, Mark, Henry, Matt, Noah, Viv (I know you're not a lad, Viv) and my very own Joe. Walk it off, lads!